How to Pass The California Driver's License Written Test

RICHARD P. CLEM

PO Box 14957

Minneapolis, MN 55414

ISBN: 1483989143
ISBN-13: 978-1483989143

INTRODUCTION: THE CALIFORNIA DRIVER'S LICENSE WRITTEN TEST

This book will help you prepare for the written test for your California driver's license or permit. If you follow the advice in this book, you **will** pass the test.

The number of questions on the test depends on your age. If you are under 18, there will be 36 questions, and you need to get at least 30 right. If you are over 18, there will be 18 questions, and you need to get at least 15 right.

The test is not difficult. In fact, most (but not all) of the questions can be answered with common sense. In fact, many of the questions are **too** easy. Therefore, the people who make the test need to make some of the questions slightly confusing to make sure that you are paying attention. This book will help you recognize the trick questions and get them right.

There are also a few questions that require you to memorize a particular answer. In most cases, these questions don't make you a safer driver. For example, to be a safe driver, you probably don't need to know the exact speed limit for driving in an alley. A safe driver knows to drive slowly, and it really doesn't matter if the exact speed limit is 14 miles per hour or 15 miles per hour. But for the test, you need to know the exact speed limit, which is 15 miles per hour. The last chapter of this book will have all of the facts that you need to memorize.

You **will** pass the test, and probably get a perfect score, if you do the following things:

1. **Read the California Driver Handbook**. You can get a free copy at any DMV office, or you can download it from the state website: For a PDF copy, go to: http://apps.dmv.ca.gov/pubs/dl600.pdf. For an HTML version,

which is better for viewing in a web browser, go to: http://www.dmv.ca.gov/pubs/hdbk/driver_handbook_toc.htm. The most important part to read is pages 16-88 of the 2013 Handbook. Read that part of the book at least once before taking the test.

2. **Read this book**. This book covers the items that are most likely to appear on the actual test. This book is divided into chapters. Some of the chapters are very short, because they cover only the material that will probably be on the test. The state is constantly changing the test, and it's always possible that new questions will be added. But if you know all of the material in this book, then you should be able to answer 99% of the questions correctly.

3. **Answer the practice questions at the end of each chapter**. The questions in this book will cover 99% of the questions on the actual test. The actual test will be multiple choice, but most of the questions in this book will be "fill in the blank". That means that the actual test will be easier. If you can answer all of the questions in this book, then you will be able to answer all of the questions on the real test. If you get any questions wrong, re-study that chapter until you get the question right.

4. **Memorize all of the information in chapter 25.**. Chapter 25 contains all of the information where you need to know the **exact** answer. Most of the questions on the test can be answered using common sense. However, in some cases, you need to know exact answers, even if knowing the exact answer doesn't make you a safer driver.

5. **Read all of the questions and answers carefully.** Most of the questions on the actual test are common sense. However, some of the questions are so simple that everyone would automatically get the answer right. For example, if a question showed you a picture of a stop sign, obviously, the correct answer would be that you need to stop. But if that was the right answer, the question would be too easy. Therefore, the correct answer will re-phrase the obvious answer, or will add

additional information. Therefore, when you see these easy questions, be especially careful when you read them. For example, there's sometimes a question about car pool lanes. The question will show a sign saying that the lane is for cars with a minimum of three people, and ask you which kind of car can drive in that lane. The correct answer is that a convertible with one adult and two children can drive there. It doesn't matter that it is a convertible, and the age of the people doesn't matter. As long as there are three people, they can drive in that lane. Therefore, don't get confused by the additional information.

6. **Take the practice tests in the Driver Handbook and the DMV website**. There are practice tests on pages 93 and 94 of the Driver Handbook, and there are also practice tests on the DMV website. After you finish this book, you should get all of those questions right. If you get any of the questions on the practice tests wrong, study those questions until you get all of the practice tests completely right. A few of the questions on the practice test will be on the real test, so you want to make sure you are able to answer all of them correctly.

When you answer the practice questions in this book, some of the "fill in the blank" questions will have more than one correct answer. For example, you might answer "slow down", but when you look at the answer, it says "take your foot off the gas." Don't worry if you don't use the exact words, as long as you recognize that your answer is right. However, the words used in the correct answer are likely to be the words used on the actual multiple-choice test. Therefore, it's important to recognize how the answer might be worded.

CONTENTS

1: DEFENSIVE DRIVING

Most of the questions on the test come under the general category of "defensive driving," and most of these questions can be answered using common sense. **Defensive driving** means that you **keep your eyes moving** looking for possible hazards. It also means that you should keep a "**space cushion**" around your vehicle. The reason for keeping a "space cushion" is to give yourself time to react if another driver makes a mistake.

Sometimes, the test will use the word "space cushion." Other times, it will give you a situation and ask you what you should do. For example, one question might ask what to do if you are driving and there are oncoming cars on your left and a row of parked cars on your right. The correct answer is that you should stay in the middle between the oncoming cars and the parked cars. In other words, you need to keep a space cushion on both sides, even though the question doesn't use those words.

If there is any question about any kind of even slightly unusual situation, then the answer is **usually** that you should **slow down and use caution**. So if there is a question about a subject that is not covered in the Driver Handbook, the answer will usually be **slow down and use caution**. So if you see zombies walking by the side of the road, you should slow down and use caution. If you witness an alien invasion while driving, you should slow down and use caution. If there is a nuclear war, you should slow down and use caution. In general, if it's a situation where there is no other specific advice that applies, you should slow down and use caution.

"Take your foot off the gas pedal" is another way of saying **"slow down"** Therefore, if it's any kind of unusual situation, the "take your foot off the gas pedal" is probably the right answer.

There is one exception to this rule, however. If you are driving a lot slower than the flow of traffic on the road, this can cause an accident. Therefore, in general, **you should not drive faster or slower than the flow traffic.** Look for the word **"flow"** in the question or answer. If the word "flow" appears, then driving too slow might cause an accident, or you could get a ticket for driving too slow. If the word "flow" does **not** appear, and it's any kind of unusual situation, then **slowing down** is probably the right answer.

The test usually has one question about **"rubbernecking"**, which means slowing down to look at an accident, a construction zone, or some other unusual thing. You have to be careful about these questions. If the question has the word "rubbernecking" and/or the word "flow," then the correct answer is probably that you should **not** slow down, because it will disrupt the flow of traffic. If you are confused by these questions, ask yourself **why** the person is slowing down. If the person is slowing down because it is safer to slow down, then the correct answer is probably to slow down. On the other hand, if the person is slowing down just because they want to look at something interesting, then the correct answer is probably that they should not slow down. If you are in doubt, look for the word "flow." If the word "flow" appears in the question or answer, then the answer is almost always that they should not slow down. If the word "flow" does not appear, then the answer is that they should probably slow down.

In other chapters, we'll learn about some of the "right-of-way" rules. If a person has the "right of way", that means that the person has the right to go first, and other cars need to wait. So in some situations that we'll talk about later, one driver has the right of way, and the other driver needs to yield. But even if the other driver has the right of way, you should let them go first if it will prevent an accident. If there is an accident, it will probably be the other person's fault, because they didn't have the right of way. But it's better just to avoid the accident in the first place. Therefore, if the test asks whether you should yield the right of way to avoid an accident, then the answer is yes.

The other side of the coin is that you should **never assume that the other driver will give you the right of way**. Again, if they crash into you, it will probably be their fault. But it's better to avoid the accident in the first place.

Another thing that is almost always the correct thing to do in any unusual situation is to **increase your following distance**, which means **increase the distance between your car and the car in front of you**. If no other answer looks right, this is almost always the correct answer. For example, one question asks you what you should do if another car is tailgating you. The correct answer to this question is to increase the distance between you and the car in front of you. This might seem like the wrong answer. After all, the car behind you is too close, so the natural reaction might be to speed up and try to get away. But if you do speed up, the car behind you will also probably speed up. Then, if the car in front of you stops suddenly, all three of you will probably get into a crash. Therefore, if you slow down slightly and make sure **you** are not tailgating, it can prevent an accident.

In general, you should always follow the **three second rule** when following other cars. This means that there should always take you at least three seconds to get to the spot where the vehicle in front of you is.

Tailgating is the opposite of driving with a safe following distance. In other words, it means driving too close to the car in front of you. You don't want to do this because it is a common **cause of rear-end collisions**.

Three seconds is how far you should be behind the car in front of you. But you also need to know what the other cars are doing. Therefore, you need to keep watching everything that's going on at least **10-15 seconds** ahead of you.

Checking your mirrors often is almost always the correct answer. Checking your mirrors is the only way you can know what's going on behind you. There are three times when it's especially important to check your mirrors. These are when you are **backing, changing lanes, or slowing down quickly.**

There will probably be a question about when you should adjust your mirrors. You should adjust your mirrors **before you start driving**.

You should check your mirrors often, and if "check your mirrors" is one of the answers, then it's probably the right answer. However, you need to know about **blind spots**. A blind spot means an area that you can't see in your mirror. Therefore, in some situations, such as **changing lanes, merging**, or **backing up**, you need to **turn your head and look over your shoulder**. Whenever you do any of these things, you need to look over your shoulder. If you are moving into the left lane, then you need to look over your left shoulder. If you are moving into the right lane, then you need to look over your right shoulder.

You also need to know about other vehicle's blind spots. If there are other cars on the road, it's best to be in front of them or behind them, and not to the side of them. This is because if you are off to their side, you are probably in their blind spot.

Backing up requires **caution**. One question asks you when backing up is dangerous. **Backing up is always dangerous**. One question asks you the things you should do before backing up. The correct answer is that you should check behind your vehicle before you get in, and you should look over your right shoulder as you back up. One of the wrong answers is that you should honk your horn. This is the wrong answer because honking the horn won't help someone who is **behind** your car.

There is usually one question on the test about when you should use your horn. You should use your horn if it will **prevent an accident**. So if there is a question about someone who can't see you, then honking the horn is probably the right answer.

There is usually one question about slowing down for a sharp curve. The important thing to remember is that when you slow down for a curve, you should slow down **before** you get to the curve. Instead of "slow down," the question might ask when you should start braking. The answer is that you should slow down or start braking **before** you get to the curve.

1-1.   The "_____-second rule" applies to the space in front of your vehicle. **Three**

1-2.   What should you do to see how traffic is moving behind you? **Check your mirrors often.**

1-3. To see potential hazards early, what should you do? **Look 10-15 seconds ahead of you.**

1- 4. When is backing up a vehicle dangerous? **Always.**

1-5. What should you do if it will prevent an accident? **Yield your legal right-of-way.**

1-6. When do collisions tend to happen? **When one vehicle is traveling faster or slower than the flow of traffic.**

1-7. You will probably interfere with the flow of traffic and get a ticket if: **you drive slower than the flow of traffic.**

1-8. You see a car approaching from the rear. When you check your mirror again to change lanes, you can't see that car. What should you do? **Look over your shoulder to make sure the car isn't in your blind spot.**

1-9. What should you do if a driver looks like he or she is going to pull out in front of you? **Slow or stop your car and use your horn.**

1-10. What will happen if you drive faster than other vehicles on a road with one lane in each direction and continually pass the other cars? **You will increase your chances of an accident.**

1-11. At intersections, crosswalks, and railroad crossings, you should always: **Look to the sides of your vehicle to see what is coming.**

1-12. You drive defensively when you _____. **Keep your eyes moving to look for possible hazards.**

1-13. What can happen when you tailgate other drivers (drive close to their rear bumper)? **You can frustrate the other drivers and make them angry.**

1-14. Why should you have a "space cushion" around your vehicle? **To give time to react if another driver makes a mistake.**

1-15. What should you do when you are near schools, playgrounds, or residential areas? **Drive more carefully.**

1- 16. What should you do if there is one lane in your direction and the vehicle ahead of you often slows down for no apparent reason? **Increase the following distance between you and other vehicle.**

1-17. It helps to improve traffic flow if you do this at an accident scene: **Not slow down to look.**

1-18. You are driving, and there are oncoming cars on your left and a row of parked cars on your right. Where should you steer? **A middle course between the oncoming and parked cars.**

1-19. Three of the most important times to check traffic behind you are before: **Backing, changing lanes, or slowing down quickly.**

1-20. What should you do if you approach a curve or the top of a hill and you do not have a clear view of the road ahead? **Slow down so you can stop if necessary.**

1-21. If you are being tailgated by another driver what should you do? **Increase the distance between your car and the one in front of you.**

1-22. When should you should use your horn? **When it may help prevent an accident.**

1-23. What are things you should do to safely back up? **Check behind your vehicle before you get in, and look over your right shoulder as you back up.**

1-24. Do you need to tap your horn before you back up? **No.**

1-25. What should you do if another car suddenly cuts in front of you can creates a hazard? **Take your foot off the gas.**

1-26. Why shouldn't you slow down just to look at accidents or other unusual things? **It causes traffic congestion.**

1-27. What should you do to see how traffic is moving behind you? **Check your mirrors often.**

1-28. You are approaching a sharp curve in the road. What should you do? **Start braking before you enter the curve.**

1-29. When should you should adjust your rear view and side view mirrors? **Before you start driving**

1-30. Why is it dangerous to drive along the right-rear side of another vehicle? **Because you're probably in one of the driver's blind spots.**

1-31. Where should you drive on a multilane street with two way traffic? **Ahead of or behind the other vehicles.**

1-32. What should you never assume about other drivers? **Never assume that they will give you the right-of-way.**

1-33. On a sharp curve, when should you use your brakes to slow your vehicle? **Before you enter the curve.**

1-34. What do you need to do to see vehicles in your blind spots? **Look over your shoulders.**

1-35. What should you do if you see a car approaching from the rear, but when you check your mirror to change lanes, you no longer see the car? **Look over your shoulder to be sure the car isn't in your blind spot.**

1-36. Why shouldn't you tailgate (follow closely behind another vehicle)? **Because it is a common cause of rear-end collisions.**

1-37. What should you do if you are approaching a sharp curve in the road? **Start braking before you enter the curve.**

1-38. What are the three most important times to check traffic behind you? **When you are backing, changing lanes, or slowing down quickly.**

1-39. What should you do if you approach a curve or the top of a hill and you do not have a clear view of the road ahead? **Slow down so you can stop if necessary.**

1-40. What do you need to do to see vehicles in your blind spots? **Turn your head.**

1-41. What should you do if you are being tailgated by another driver? **Increase the distance between your car and the vehicle ahead.**

1-42. What should you do if you see a vehicle stopped on the right shoulder of the road ahead with its hazard lights on? **Slow down and**

pass very carefully.

2: SEAT BELTS

There are always one or two questions on the test about seat belts, but there are only a few facts you need to know.

1. If your car has seat belts, then you are required to wear them. Sometimes, the wrong answers will give the age of the vehicle. For example, if you are driving a 1930 Model T, it probably doesn't have seat belts. But for the test, you don't need to know the age of the vehicle. If the vehicle does have seat belts, then you need to wear them.
2. If your car also has a separate shoulder belt, then you are also required to wear it.
3. If you don't wear seat belts, you can get a traffic ticket.
4. If a passenger under 16 years old is not wearing a seat belt, then the driver can also get a ticket.
5. If the car has airbags, then you are safest if you are least 10 inches away from the steering wheel.
6. Seat belts increase your chances of surviving an accident.
7. Children under 6 years old are required to be in an approved car seat. There is only one exception: If the child weighs more than 60 pounds, then they don't need to be in a car seat, but they do need to wear the seat belt.
8. The test is 100% in favor of seat belts. If any answer says anything bad about seat belts, then the answer is wrong.

Finally, there is one "trick question" about seat belts. California does not have a specific law saying that people can't ride in the back of a pickup truck. However, everyone is required to wear a seatbelt, and I have never seen a pickup truck with seatbelts in the back. So if someone is riding in the back of a pickup truck, they will probably get a ticket for not wearing a seat belt. Therefore, if you get a question of when it's legal to ride in the back of a pickup truck, the correct answer is that you can, but only **if you are secured in a seat and using an approved safety belt.**

Finally, some of the questions use the words "safety belt," and some use the words "seat belt." They both mean the same thing.

2-1. If you are riding in a vehicle with a lap belt and also a separate shoulder belt what are you required to do? **Use both the lap belt and shoulder belt.**

2-2. When are you are required to use your seat belt? **Whenever you are in a vehicle that is equipped with seat belts.**

2-3. If you don't wear your safety belt in a moving vehicle, what will happen? **You will receive a traffic ticket.**

2-4. If a passenger is younger than 16 and is not wearing a seat belt, what will happen? **The driver can receive a citation.**

2-5. If your car has air bags, where are you safest? **At least 10 inches away from the steering wheel.**

2-6. What is true about safety belts and collisions? **Safety belts increase your chances of survival in most types of collisions.**

2-7. All children under age six riding in your vehicle must use a child passenger restraint system unless: **They weigh 60 pounds or more and wear a safety belt.**

2-8. The only time you can legally ride in the back of a pickup truck is:
If you are secured in a seat and using an approved safety belt.

3: EMERGENCY VEHICLES

There is usually one question on the test about emergency vehicles. The main thing you need to know is that if you see an emergency vehicle with flashing lights behind you, you need to **drive as near to the right edge of the road as possible and stop.** If you are crossing an intersection when you see the emergency vehicle, then you should **continue through the intersection** before you stop. The reason why you need to do this is because you don't know if the emergency vehicle is going to turn. If you stop in the intersection, then you might be in the way.

Finally, you probably know that if the police are chasing you, you should stop. For the test, you need to know that if you don't stop and someone gets seriously injured, then you can be sent to the state prison for up to **seven years.**

3-1. You are being chased by a police vehicle with its light and sirens activated. You ignore the warning to stop and speed away. During the chase, a person is seriously injured. What is the penalty? **Imprisonment in a state prison for up to seven years**

3-2. What should you do if you see an emergency vehicle with flashing lights behind you? **Drive as near to the right edge of the road as possible and stop.**

3-3. What should you do if you are crossing an intersection and an emergency vehicle is approaching with a siren and flashing lights? **Continue through the intersection, pull to the right, and stop.**

4: CELL PHONES AND HEADPHONES

There is almost always one question on the test about cell phones, and sometimes about listening to headphones. The only things you need to know for the test are:

1. When using cell phones while driving, you should use a **hands-free device** so that you can keep both hands on the wheel.
2. There is only one exception: You can use a cell phone without a hands-free device **only when making a call for emergency assistance.**
3. If the phone rings while you are driving (and you don't have a hands-free device), then you should not answer it. On the test, the correct answer almost always says "**you should let the call go to voice mail.**"
4. It is illegal and dangerous to use **headphones that cover both ears**. Sometimes, the test calls these "dual headphones."

4-1. The safest precaution that you can take regarding the use of cell phones when driving is: **Use hands-free devices so you can keep both hands on the steering wheel.**

4-2. It is illegal and dangerous to do what while driving? **Listen to music through headphones that cover both ears.**

4-3. When is it legal to use a cell phone without a hands-free device while driving? **Only when making a call for emergency assistance.**

4-4. What should you do if your cell phone rings while you are driving and you do not have a hands-free device? **Let the call go to voicemail.**

5: LANE MARKINGS

There are always a few question on the test about lane markings. The first thing you need to know is that **yellow** is always the color used to separate cars traveling in opposite directions. Therefore, if there is any kind of yellow line, this means that it is a two-way road. If it is a yellow **broken line**, this means that cars are allowed to pass in either direction.

If it is a **double yellow line** that is solid on both sides, this means that it is illegal to pass for cars going in either direction. If it's a **broken yellow line** on one side and a **solid yellow line** on the other side, this means that it's illegal to pass if the solid yellow line is on your side.

Even if there is a double yellow line, you are allowed to cross the line **if you are making a left turn**. But you are not allowed to cross the line **to pass**.

If there are **two sets of double yellow lines** (two feet or more apart), this means that you can **never** cross the lines for any reason. You have to treat those lines as if they were a **solid wall**.

Be careful when you read these questions. Usually, the question will use the words "next to the broken line" when it's OK to pass. The question will usually use the words "next to the solid line" when it's illegal to pass.

5-1. If there is a double solid yellow line dividing opposite lanes of traffic, when may you cross the lines? **To make a left turn from or into a side street.**

5-2. When can you cross two sets of solid, double, yellow lines that are two or more feet apart? **Never. You may not cross them for any reason.**

5-3. When may you may cross a double, yellow line to pass another vehicle? **If the yellow line next to your side of the road is a broken line.**

5-4. A solid yellow line next to a broken yellow line means that vehicles next to the broken line may do what? **Pass other vehicles.**

5-5. You are not allowed to cross double solid yellow lines in the center of the roadway to ___. **Pass other vehicles.**

5-6. Two sets of solid double yellow lines (more than two feet apart) should be treated the same as what? **A solid wall and never crossed.**

5-7. If there are two solid yellow lines in the center of the road, are you allowed to cross the lines to turn left into a driveway? **Yes.**

5-8. What do solid yellow lines separate? **Vehicles traveling in opposite directions.**

5-9. What do yellow lines separate? **Traffic moving in opposite directions on a two-way road.**

6: HEADLIGHTS AND NIGHT DRIVING

The test will almost always have a few questions on the use of headlights. On these questions, keep in mind that there are some numbers that you need to memorize. Obviously, you should use your headlights at night. In fact, at night, you should use your **high-beams whenever it is legal and safe to use them** because the high-beams will allow you to see the maximum distance. However, there are two times when you need to switch to your low-beam headlights. If there is an oncoming vehicle, you need to dim the lights when you are within **500 feet**. If there is a vehicle in front of you, you should dim them when you are within **300 feet**. You should memorize both of these numbers, because they will probably be on the test.

There's an easy way to remember which is which. An oncoming car will be looking at you all the time, so it's more important not to blind them. Therefore, you need to dim your lights for them when you are further away, 500 feet. It's also important not to shine your high-beam lights on the car in front of you, but it's not quite as important. The person in front of you can still see the road, and your high-beams will only bother them if they are looking in their rear-view mirror. Therefore, it's OK to get a little bit closer to them, 300 feet.

If an oncoming driver forgets to turn off their high-beams, it's important that you not get blinded by looking at them. Therefore, what you should do is keep your eyes on the right side of your lane.

When you are driving at night, you always want to make sure that you have time to stop if you see something in the road. Therefore, on a dark street, you should drive slowly enough so that **you can stop within the area lighted by your headlights**.

You are usually not **required** to have your headlights on during the day, but there is nothing wrong with having them on. During the day, you should use the low-beams.

You are **never** allowed to drive with just your parking lights turned on.

6-1. Using low beams during the day on narrow country roads is: **A proper use of your vehicle lights.**

6-2. You are driving at night on a dimly lit street and using high beams. You should dim your lights when you are within _____ of an oncoming vehicle. **500 feet.**

6-3. When driving in traffic at night on a dimly lit street, you should drive slowly enough so that _____. **You can stop within the area lighted by your headlights.**

6-4. You are driving at night on a dimly lit street and using high beams. You should dim your lights when you are within _____ of a vehicle you are approaching from behind. **300 feet.**

6-5. If an oncoming vehicle fails to dim its high beams, what should you do? **Look toward the right edge of your lane.**

6-6. At night, when should you use your high-beam headlights? **Whenever it is legal and safe.**

6-7. When are you allowed to drive using only your parking lights?
Never.

7: TRUCKS, BICYCLES, MOTORCYCLES, TRAILERS

There are always questions about sharing the road with trucks, bicycles, or motorcycles. Sometimes, there is a question about you towing a trailer.

If one of the answers to a question is to allow extra room in front of your car, then this is probably the right answer. You need to allow extra room if a motorcycle is in front of you, because the motorcycle can stop faster. You need to allow extra room for a large truck or bus because it can block your vision.

Remember the following facts about trucks, because one of them will probably be on the test: Trucks often appear to travel more slowly than they are really going, because of their large size. Trucks take longer to stop than cars; therefore, they often travel with more space in front of them. Trucks usually have a larger blind spot than cars. When a truck is turning, it might need to swing wide (use more than one lane). Trucks are likely to lose speed going up a hill, which might cause a hazard. Finally, trucks carrying hazardous cargo are always required to stop before crossing a railroad track. You can tell these trucks because they have a hazardous material placard, which is a diamond-shaped sign, on the back.

When passing a bicycle, you need to allow enough room. Normally, this is at least 3 feet. If there's an oncoming car, you might need to wait for the car to go by before you pass the bicycle.

A bicycle lane is normally at the right side of the road. If you need to turn right, you need to merge into the bicycle lane before making your turn. This is the only time you are allowed to drive in the bicycle lane, and you are only allowed to drive there for 200 feet before the turn. But bicycles are allowed to share the road, so they might be in the normal traffic lanes with you.

Always watch carefully for bicycles, because they might be in your blind spot.

There is usually only one question about motorcycles. You need to know that motorcycles have the same rights and responsibilities as other vehicles.

If you are towing a trailer, the maximum speed limit is 55 mph, and you need to stay in the right lane. There is one exception, and that exception is on the test. If there are four or more lanes in your direction, then you can drive in either of the two right lanes.

7-1. If you are towing another vehicle or trailer on a freeway with four lanes in your direction, where may you may travel? **Either of the two right lanes.**

7- 2. What should you do if you are following a large tour bus? **Allow extra space in front of your vehicle.**

7-3. If you want to pass a bicyclist riding on the right edge of your lane, what should you do? **Allow a minimum of 3 feet between you and the cyclist.**

7-4. You want to pass a bicyclist in a narrow traffic lane, and an oncoming car is approaching. What should you do? **Slow down and let the car pass, then pass the bicyclist.**

7-5. If you want to turn right and your driving lane is next to a bicycle lane, what should you do? **Merge into the bicycle lane before making your turn.**

7-6. You are driving on the freeway. The vehicle in front of you is a large truck. Where should you drive? **Further behind the truck than you would for a passenger vehicle.**

7-7. Why do you need more space in front of your vehicle when following a large truck? **Because you need the extra room to see around the truck.**

7-8. When can you drive in a bike lane? **When you are within 200 feet of a cross street where you plan to turn right.**

7-9. What is true about the apparent speed of large trucks? **Trucks often appear to travel more slowly because of their large size.**

7-10. Large trucks take _____ than passenger cars. **Longer to stop.**

7-11. What is true about motorcyclists and motorists? **Motorcyclists have the same rights and responsibilities as other motorists.**

7-12. If a vehicle is displaying a diamond-shaped sign, then it must _____. **Stop before crossing railroad tracks.**

7-13. What is true about blind spots in trucks? **Large trucks have bigger blind spots than most passenger vehicles.**

7-14. Why do large trucks often travel with a lot of space in front of them? **Because the truck driver needs to use the extra space for stopping the vehicle.**

7-15. What kind of vehicle must always stop before crossing railroad tracks? **Tank trucks marked with hazardous materials placards.**

7-16. A large truck is ahead of you and is turning right onto a street with two lanes in each direction. What might happen? **The truck may have to swing wide to complete the right turn.**

7-17. If a truck is turning right, what might happen? **It might use part of the left lane to complete the turn.**

7-18. When might a large truck lose speed and cause a hazard? **Going up long or steep hills.**

7-19. Why must you carefully watch for bicycles in traffic lanes? **Because they could be hidden in your blind spots.**

7-20. Why can bicycles sometimes use the same lanes used by motor vehicles? **Because they are entitled to share the road with you.**

8: SIGNS

The test will show you pictures of signs and ask what they mean. You should look at all of the signs on pages 22-27 of the Driver Handbook and make sure you are familiar with all of them. The ones shown below are the most likely to be on the test, but it's possible that other signs might appear.

When you see questions about signs, you need to remember that most of these questions are very easy. For example, a stop sign means that you need to stop. But if the question was worded that way, it would be too easy. Therefore, these questions are the most likely to contain additional information, or be worded in a complicated way. So pay close attention to these "easy" questions.

This sign means that you can't enter the road from your direction.

You can't pass other vehicles for any reason.

There is a traffic signal ahead.

There is a pedestrian crossing ahead.

You need to give the right-of-way to other drivers. Sometimes, the answer is worded "give the right-of-way to traffic on the road you wish to enter or cross." The answer will almost always have the words "give the right-of-way". It really means "yield the right-of-way", but if they used that word, the question would be too easy.

Another road crosses your road ahead.

If you see this sign, you need to be prepared to stop if children are in the crosswalk.

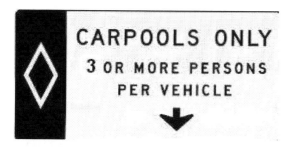

For this question, you will probably be given more information than you need, and you will be asked whether a certain car can use the lane. For example, one version of the question asks whether it's OK to use this lane if you are driving a convertible with one adult and two children. The answer is that you can use the lane, because there are three people. It doesn't matter how old they are, and it doesn't matter what kind of car they have. One of the wrong answers has one person and two animals. This vehicle can't use the lane, because there are not three people in the car. The people need to be humans, not animals.

You may not enter the road from your direction.

If the light is green, you can turn left if it is safe.

You are approaching a railroad crossing. Prepare to stop if necessary.

You must stop and check traffic in all directions before proceeding

This sign on a vehicle means that it is a slow-moving vehicle.

This sign means that you should look, listen, and prepare to stop at the crossing, if necessary.

The right lane will end ahead

Vehicles on this road travel in two directions

There is a sharp turn to the right.

There is road work ahead. Remember, **orange** signs always mean construction.

For the questions in this chapter, tell what the sign means.

8-1.

You may not enter the road from your direction

8-2.

You can't pass other vehicles for any reason.

8-3.

There is a traffic signal ahead.

8-4.

There is a pedestrian crosswalk ahead

8-5.

You should give the right-of-way to traffic on the road you wish to

enter or cross

8-6.

You must give the right-of-way to other drivers.

8-7.

Another road crosses yours ahead.

8-8.

You should be prepared to stop if children are in the crosswalk.

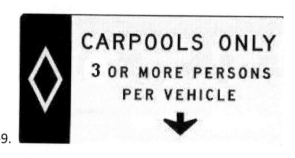

8-9.

Which example is given on the test of a car that's allowed to use this lane? **A convertible with an adult and two children.**

8-10.

There is a pedestrian crossing ahead.

8-11.

You may not enter the road from your direction.

8-12.

You may turn left on a green light when it is safe.

8-13.

You are approaching a railroad crossing. Prepare to stop.

8-14.

You should stop and check traffic in all directions before proceeding.

8-15.   What does this sign mean on a vehicle:

It is a slow-moving vehicle.

8-16.

Look, listen, and prepare to stop at the crossing, if necessary.

8-17.

The right lane will end ahead.

8-18.

Vehicles on this road travel in two directions.

8-19.

There is a sharp turn to the right.

8-20.

There is road work ahead.

9: CONSTRUCTION

There will be one or two questions on the test about driving through construction areas. To get these questions right, here are the facts you need to know:

1. In a construction zone, **you are responsible** for the safety of the workers.
2. **Orange signs** mean that you are in or near a construction area.
3. In a construction zone, you should **slow down and be prepared to stop.**
4. You should **avoid "rubbernecking"** in a construction zone.
5. If there is a **flagger** or **signal person**, you need to obey their instructions at all times.

9-1. You see a signal person at a road construction site ahead. What do you need to do? **Obey his or her instructions at all times.**

9-2. In a construction zone, who is responsible for the safety of the road workers? **You are.**

9-3. What should you do when you are driving near construction zones? **Reduce speed and be prepared to stop.**

9-4. At a construction site, you are always required to obey instructions from _____. **Flaggers (signal persons).**

9-5. When driving near road construction zones, what should you do? **Pass the construction zone carefully and avoid "rubbernecking."**

9-6. _____-colored road signs warn you of road workers or road equipment ahead. **Orange.**

10: INTERSECTIONS AND TRAFFIC LIGHTS

There's almost always one question on the test about blocking an intersection. You never want to get stuck in an intersection after your light turns red, because then you will be blocking the traffic going the other way. You can **never** legally block an intersection. This is one question where you usually get extra information to confuse you. For example, the question might ask if you can block the intersection if you have a green light, or if it is rush hour. The answer is always no, no matter how much extra information you are given. You can never block an intersection.

Therefore, if the light is green, but there is traffic stuck in the intersection, you should wait and not enter the intersection until you can get through. Also, if you are waiting and the light turns green, you need to wait if there are still other cars in the intersection. And remember, when the light turns green, you need to **look** before you go. You need to look to the **left**, then to the **right**, and then to the **left again**.

If you are driving and the light turns **yellow**, then you should stop before entering the intersection, if you can do so safely. If you can't stop safely, then you should enter the intersection cautiously and continue across.

Obviously, if the light is **red**, then you are supposed to stop. There is sometimes a question on the test about one exception: If a police officer signals you to continue driving through the red light, then you should do as the officer tells you.

When you stop at an intersection, if there is no crosswalk or limit line, then the correct place to stop is at the corner.

If the light is **flashing red**, this means the same thing as a stop sign. You need to stop until it is safe to go. You also need to stop if you come to a traffic signal that is not working (blacked out). This is also the same as a stop sign: You need to stop until it is safe to go.

A **flashing yellow light** (at an intersection or anywhere else) always means **caution**. At an intersection, this means that you should slow down, be alert, and cross the intersection carefully.

In California, you are allowed to turn right if the light is red (unless there's a sign that says you can't). But before you turn, you need to **come to a complete stop**.

If there is a **red arrow** pointing in some direction, this means that you can't turn that direction until the light turns green. There's one trick question on the test that asks what the difference is between a red light and a red arrow pointing. The answer that they are looking for is that "if there is a red arrow, you are not allowed to turn, even if you stop first." When you think about it, this makes sense. If there's a red light, you can make a right turn after you stop. But if there's a red arrow pointing that direction, you're not allowed to turn until the red arrow is gone.

There is also a trick question about **yellow arrows**: If you are going to make a left turn from the left-turn lane and the yellow arrow appears, then you need to be prepared to obey the next signal that appears. "The next signal that appears" is probably going to be a red arrow, and the question would be less confusing if they worded it that way. But that's not how they worded it, so watch out for that question.

An **uncontrolled intersection** is one that doesn't have any stop signs or stop lights. When you come to an uncontrolled intersection, you should slow down and be ready to stop if necessary.

There might be a question on the test about who has the right-of-way at an intersection if more than one car gets there at the same time. If it's a four-way intersection, the car on the right has the right-of-way. Read this question carefully. If it says the other car is to your left, it means that you have the right-of-way, because you are to that car's right. If it's a "T" intersection and there are no stop signs or light, then the car on the through street has the right-of-way.

10-1. What should you do when a light turns yellow? **You should stop before entering the intersection, if you can do so safely.**

10-2. When approaching an intersection at the posted speed limit when the signal light turns yellow, what should you do? **Stop before entering the intersection, if you can do so safely**

10-3. If you are going to make a left turn from the left-turn lane and the yellow arrow appears, what should you do? **Be prepared to obey the next signal that appears.**

10-4. Where should you stop your vehicle if there is no crosswalk or limit line? **At the corner.**

10-5. If a police officer signals you to continue driving through a red light, what should you do? **Do as the officer tells you.**

10-6. You are approaching an intersection at the posted speed limit when the signal light turns yellow. What should you do? **Stop before entering the intersection, if you can do so safely.**

10-7. Is it legal to block an intersection during rush hour if you have the green light? **No.**

10-8. When can you legally turn right on a solid red light? **Only after stopping, unless otherwise posted.**

10-9. for which traffic lights must you always stop your vehicle? **Solid red lights, flashing red lights, and blacked-out traffic signals.**

10-10. On a traffic light, what does it mean if a red arrow is pointing to the right? **You may not turn that direction until the light turns green.**

10-11. What should you do if a traffic signal light isn't working at an intersection? **You should come to a complete stop then proceed when it is safe.**

10-12. What is the difference between a traffic light with a red arrow and one with a red light? **If there is a red arrow, you are not allowed to turn, even if you stop first.**

10-13. When may you legally block an intersection? **Under no circumstances.**

10-14. If you have a green light, but traffic is blocking the intersection, what should you do? **Stay out of the intersection until traffic clears.**

10-15. You see a flashing yellow traffic signal at an upcoming intersection. What does the flashing yellow light mean? **Slow down and cross the intersection carefully.**

10-16. What should you do if you approach an intersection without a stop sign or signals? **Slow down and be ready to stop if necessary.**

10-17. You reach an intersection with stop signs on all four corners at the same time as another the driver on your left. Who has the right of way? **You do.**

10-18. What does a flashing yellow traffic signal at an intersection mean? **Slow down and be alert at the intersection.**

10-19. What does a flashing red light at an intersection mean? **Stop before entering.**

10-20. Two vehicles are approaching an uncontrolled "T" intersection. One vehicle is on the through road, and the other is on the road that ends. Who has the right-of-way at the intersection? **The vehicle on the through road.**

10-21. What should you do if you have a green light, but traffic is blocking the intersection? **Stay out of the intersection and wait until traffic clears.**

10-22. You should never start across an intersection if you know _____. **you will block the intersection when the light turns red.**

10-23. What should you do if you approach an intersection without a stop sign or signals? **Slow down and be ready to stop if necessary.**

10-24. You are stopped at an intersection, and the traffic light just turned green. Should you go immediately? **No. You must wait until other vehicles clear the intersection before you enter.**

10-25. Before driving into an intersection from a stop, you should look _____. **Left, right, and left again.**

10-26. If you cannot stop safely at a yellow traffic light, what should you do? **Enter the intersection cautiously and continue across.**

10-27. What should you do if you are approaching an uncontrolled intersection? **Slow down and be ready to stop.**

11: TURNS

There will almost always be one question on the test asking about turns. This question will ask you what lane you should be in when you start the turn, and what lane you should be in when you finish turning. These questions are very easy. If you are turning **left**, then you start in the lane that is furthest **left**, and you finish the turn in the lane that is the furthest **left**. If you are turning **right**, then you start in the lane that is furthest **right**, and you finish the turn in the lane that is the furthest **right**.

This is so simple that the people who made the test need to turn it into a trick question. The only way to do this is to re-word it so that it is more confusing. Therefore, the question will probably describe the lane with words like "left lane for traffic in your direction," "the lane closest to the left curb," "the lane closest to the right curb," "the lane closest to the curb or the edge of the highway." Don't worry about these extra words. Just remember that when you turn right, you start in the right lane and finish in the right lane. When you turn left, you start in the left lane and finish in the left lane.

Sometimes, there is a trick question about turning onto a one-way street. These questions are so simple that you might think you are missing something. But you are not. The question will ask something like, "when is the only time that you can make a left turn onto a one-way street?" The correct answer is that you can turn only if the traffic on the street you're turning onto is traveling to the left. Think about this for a minute, and you'll see how simple this question is. You're turning onto a one-way street. If you are turning left, and the traffic is going right, that means that you're going the wrong way! So obviously, you can only turn onto a street if you're going the right way.

You need to remember that any time you turn left, it is potentially dangerous, because you need to cross the traffic that is coming toward you. Therefore, when making a left turn, you always need to **yield the right-of-way to cars coming toward you**.

In California (and most other states), it is OK to make a **right turn on a red light** (unless a sign says that you can't). But before you turn, you need to do two things. First of all, you need to come to a **complete stop** before starting your turn. Second, you need to **yield the right-of-way to any pedestrians**.

There is also one time when you can make a **left turn on a red light**. That is when you are turning **from** a one-way street **onto** another one-way street. And obviously, you can't be going the wrong way on either of those streets. The same rules apply as for a right turn on red: You need to stop first, and you need to yield to pedestrians.

You need to signal your turns. You should start signaling **100 feet** before the turn. You should continue signaling as you make the turn. By having your turn signal on, other drivers will know your intentions. You should always use your turn signals, even when nobody else is around.

A center left-turn lane is marked like this:

You can drive in this center lane only to start or complete a left-turn (or a legal U-turn).

11-1. If you are driving on a two-way street and you want to turn left at an upcoming corner, what do you need to do? **Give the right-of-way to vehicles coming toward you.**

11-2. You can make a right turn at a solid red light if the following three things are true: **1. You check for pedestrians and other traffic; 2. you stop first; and 3. there is no sign to prohibit the turn.**

11-3. You are on a two-way street with two lanes in each direction. To turn left, where do you start the turn? **The left lane for traffic in your direction.**

11-4. You are about to make a left turn. You must signal continuously during the last _____ feet before the turn. **100 feet.**

11-5. Why should you continuously signal while turning? **Because it lets other drivers know what your intentions are.**

11-6. To turn left from a multilane one-way street onto a one-way street, what lane should you turn from? **The lane closest to the left curb.**

11-7. You want to make a right turn at an upcoming intersection. How far ahead should you start signaling? **100 feet before turning.**

11-8. Using your turn signal at least ___ feet before turning can help you avoid _____. **100 feet, getting hit from behind.**

11-9. You are getting ready to make a right turn. What should you do first? **Slow down or stop, if necessary, and then make the turn.**

11-10. You are driving on a one-way street. You may turn left onto another one-way street only if: **The traffic on that street moves to the left.**

11-11. To turn left from a one way street with multiple lanes onto a two way street, where should you start the turn? **The far left lane.**

11-12. You are getting ready to make a right turn. You should _____ signal during the last ____ feet before you turn. **Signal, 100.**

11-13. To turn left from a one-way street, where should you start from? **The lane closest to the left curb.**

11-14. You may make a left turn on a red light only from a _____ onto _____. **One-way street, another one-way street.**

11-15. To make a right turn from a two-way street onto another two-way street, you should: **start in the right-hand lane (the lane closest to the curb), and also end in right-hand lane (the lane closest to the curb).**

11-16. It is a good habit to signal continuously during the last _____ before you turn at an intersection, even if you do not see any other vehicles around. **100 feet.**

11-17. You are getting ready to make a right turn. You must signal during the last _____ before your turn. **100 feet.**

11-18. When you want to turn left at an upcoming corner, you must give the right-of-way to _____. **All approaching vehicles.**

11-19. You enter a designated turn lane to make a left turn at an upcoming intersection. There is oncoming traffic. What do you need to do? **Signal before you arrive at the intersection.**

11-20. You want to turn left ahead. In the middle of the road, there is a lane marked as shown:

Before you turn, what do you need to do? **Merge completely into that lane.**

11-21. What is the lane in the middle of a two-way street used for? **Begin or end left turns, or start a permitted U-turn.**

11-22. If you are making a right turn from a highway with two lanes in your direction, what lane should you turn from? **The lane closest to the curb or the edge of the highway.**

12: U-TURNS

The test almost always has one question about U-turns. All you need to remember are the following four facts:

1. A U-turn is legal on a highway **if there is a paved opening for a turn**.
2. A U-turn is legal at an **intersection with a green light**, unless there is a sign saying that you can't make a U-turn.
3. In a business district, a U-turn is legal **only** at an intersection (unless there's a sign saying that you can't make a U-turn.)
4. If there's more than one lane, you always start the U-turn in the furthest possible lane to the left.

12-1. Name one legal U-turn? **On a highway where there is a paved opening for a turn.**

12-2. Unless prohibited by a sign, where can you may legally make a U-turn? **At an intersection with a green light.**

12-3. In a business district, where can you legally make a U-turn? **Only at intersections, unless a sign prohibits them.**

12-4. You are driving on a divided street with multiple lanes in your direction. If you need to make a U-turn, where should you start? **In the left lane.**

13: PARKING

Never leave your car running unattended. This means that if you need to go into a store quickly, you need to park the car properly. This means that you need to turn off the engine and set the parking brake.

When you park parallel to the curb, your wheels must be within **18 inches** of the curb.

The questions about parking on a hill are sometimes confusing, but they are not difficult when you think about them. First of all, when you park on a hill, it's especially important to set the **parking brake** and put the transmission in **park** (or leave it in gear, if it has a manual transmission). The confusing part is where to turn your wheels if you are parked on a hill. The question will tell you whether you are pointing uphill or downhill, and it will also tell you whether or not there is a curb. From that information, you can figure out where to turn the wheels. When you think about the rules, you should be able to remember them without memorizing.

The main thing to think about is what will happen if the car starts to roll away. If that happens, how you turned the wheels will prevent damage. **If there is a curb, you always point the wheels so that they will hit the curb if the car starts moving**. If the car starts to roll away, the wheel will bump into the curb, which will stop the car. That means that if you are pointing uphill with a curb, you need to turn the wheels away from the curb. (If you are parked on the right side of the street, turn the steering wheel to the left.) Think about it: The car is pointing uphill, so if it starts to roll away, it will go backwards. If the wheels are turned away from the curb, this means that the back of the wheel is turned toward the curb. The car will roll a few inches, and then bump into the curb, which will stop it.

If the car is pointing downhill, then you need to turn the wheels toward the curb. (If you are parked on the right side of the street, turn the steering wheel to the right.) If the car starts to roll away, it will go forward. The car will roll a few inches, and then bump into the curb, which will stop it.

If there is no curb, then you always turn your wheels toward the side of the road. (If you're parked on the right side of the street, then turn the steering wheel to the right.) Without a curb, there is nothing to stop the car. But if the wheels are pointing to the side, then the car will roll off the road, and this will cause less damage than if it rolls into the street.

If you think about why you are turning the wheels, you will always get these questions right. However, if you want to just memorize this information, here's what you need to know for the test:

Uphill with curb: Turn the steering wheel toward the center of the road.

Downhill with curb: Turn the steering wheel toward the side of the road.

No curb: Always turn the steering wheel toward the side of the road.

When you're parked on a level surface, then your wheels should be pointing straight ahead.

You need to know what the different colors of curbs mean. Here are the different colors the curb can be painted, and what they mean:

White Curb: Only stop to drop off passengers or mail.

Green Curb: You can park for a limited time. There will be a sign telling how long.

Yellow Curb: Only stop to load or unload passengers or freight.

Red Curb: No stopping, standing, or parking.

Blue Curb: Parking for disabled persons only. You need a placard or special license plates to park here.

Crosshatched (diagonal) lines are used to show a spot where it is illegal to park.

When parking next to a curb you should always use your turn signals. Use them when pulling next to the curb. And when you leave the parking spot, use them when you pull away from the curb.

Before getting out of your car, you should look for cars or bicycles on the traffic side of your vehicle. And when you pull away from the curb, you need a large enough gap to get up to the speed of traffic. Even if you have to wait a long time, you need to wait and yield to traffic in the lane you are moving into.

It is always illegal to park your vehicle in a crosswalk. It doesn't matter if the crosswalk is unmarked. You're still not allowed to park there.

13-1. If you want to go into a store to make a quick purchase, what should you do? **Stop the engine and set the parking brake.**

13-2. What does a curb painted blue mean? **Parking is allowed only for disabled persons with special plates or placard.**

13-3. When you park your car on any hill, what do you need to do? **Always set your parking brake and leave your vehicle in gear or the "park" position.**

13-4. When parking your vehicle parallel to the curb on a level street, your wheels must be within _____ of the curb. **18 inches.**

13-5. When parking downhill on a two-way road with no curb, turn your front wheels ____. **Right (toward the side of the road).**

13-6. What should you do if you were parked and have been waiting a long time in heavy traffic with your turn signal on to re-enter traffic? **Continue waiting and yielding to traffic in the lane.**

13-7. When parking next to a curb, when should you use your turn signals? **When pulling next to or away from the curb.**

13-8. When parking downhill next to a curb, how should you turn your front wheels? **Into the curb.**

13-9. When is parking permitted in a cross-hatched (diagonal) pattern space? **Never.**

13-10. You park your car at the curb on a level two-way street. Before getting out of your car, what should you do? Look **for cars or bicycles on the traffic side of your car.**

13-11. A white painted curb means _____. **Loading zone for passengers or mail only.**

13-12. When parking uphill on a two-way street with no curbs, your front wheels should be _____. **Turned to the right (away from the street).**

13-13. When parked uphill next to a curb, your front wheels should be _____. **Turned away from the curb.**

13-14. When may you park next to a red painted curb? **Never.**

13-15. Is it legal to park your vehicle in an unmarked crosswalk? **No.**

13-16. Your wheels should be pointed straight ahead, unless you are
_____. **Parked on a hill or sloping driveway.**

13-17. If you enter traffic from a stop (for example, pulling away from
the curb) you need _____. **A large enough gap to get up to the
speed of traffic.**

13-18. Turn your front wheels toward the curb when you park _____.
Facing downhill.

14: TRAINS

There will be at least one question on the test about railroad crossings.

You need to stop before crossing railroad tracks if a train might be approaching, even if you can't see it. At a railroad crossing, you need to **look, listen, and prepare to stop if necessary.** You can **never** go around or under a railroad crossing gate.

Never stop on railroad tracks. If you're not sure you can get all the way across, you should stop and wait before you cross the tracks.

The test sometimes has a question about light rail vehicles. The two things you need to know are: You should never turn in front of a light rail vehicle. When sharing the road with a light rail vehicle, you should monitor all traffic signals closely, because light rail vehicles can interrupt traffic signals.

14-1. When should you stop before crossing railroad tracks? **Any time a train may be approaching, whether or not you can see it.**

14-2. When sharing the road with a light rail vehicle, what should you never do? **Turn in front of an approaching light rail vehicle.**

14-3.   What does this sign mean?

Look, listen, and prepare to stop at the crossing, if necessary.

14-4. When can you legally go around or under a railroad crossing gate? **Never.**

14-5. When should you stop before you cross railroad tracks ? **You don't have room on the other side to completely cross the tracks.**

14-6. You must stop at the intersection ahead. Just before the intersection, you need to cross railroad tracks. What should you do? **Stop before the tracks if you don't have room to completely cross the tracks.**

14-7. What should you do when sharing the road with a light rail vehicle? **Monitor all traffic signals closely because light rail vehicles can interrupt traffic signals.**

15: ALCOHOL AND DRUGS

You already know that you shouldn't drink and drive. Here are the specific things you need to know about drugs and alcohol that will be on the test. You need to memorize all of the numbers, because those numbers will probably be on the test.

1. For someone 21 or over, it is illegal to operate a vehicle with a blood alcohol concentration of **0.08%** or higher.
2. For someone under 21, it is illegal to operate a vehicle with a blood alcohol concentration of **0.01%** or higher.
3. If you are convicted of driving above those limits, you can be sentenced to **six months** in jail.
4. If you are driving a motor vehicle in California, you have consented to take a chemical test for the alcohol content of your blood, breath, or urine, **any time you are asked by law enforcement.**
5. Alcohol affects your judgment, which you need to drive safely.
6. **All** medications, even over-the-counter drugs, can affect your driving ability. **You** are responsible for knowing how they affect you.
7. Most cold medicines can make you drowsy.
8. It is illegal to have an open bottle of any kind of alcohol in your car. There is an exception if it is locked in your **trunk**.
9. It is illegal to smoke in a car if there are people under 18 years old in the car. There are no exceptions.

15-1. It is illegal to drive with a blood alcohol concentration (BAC) that is ____. **0.08% or higher.**

15-2. If you are driving in California, you have consented to what? **To take a chemical test for the alcohol content of your blood, breath, or urine if asked by a law enforcement.**

15-3. What is the most important thing to remember about drinking alcohol and driving? **Alcohol affects your judgment, which you need for driving safely.**

15-4. Whose responsibility is it to know how your medications affect your driving? **Yours.**

15-5. Smoking inside a vehicle when a person younger than 18 years of age is present is_____. **Illegal at all times.**

15-6. If you are convicted of driving with an excessive blood alcohol concentration (BAC), you may be sentenced to _____. **Up to six months in jail.**

15-7. Can over-the-counter drugs can impair your driving? **Yes.**

15-8. What can most cold medications do? **Make you drowsy.**

15-9. When can you should drive under the influence of any medication that impairs your driving? **Never.**

15-10. When is it illegal to smoke inside a vehicle? **Any time a person younger than 18 years of age is present.**

15-11. When is it legal to drive with an open alcoholic beverage container? **If it is in the trunk.**

15-12. If you are under 21 years of age to drive with a blood alcohol concentration (BAC) that is _____. **0.01% or more.**

16: PEDESTRIANS

Pedestrians always have the right-of-way at crosswalks, or at intersections, even if the intersection doesn't have a marked crosswalk. You always have to wait until the pedestrian has finished crossing the street. If there's a question on the test about a pedestrian, and you're not sure of the correct answer, the correct answer almost always says that you need to yield to the pedestrian, or wait until all of the pedestrians have crossed.

A **safety zone** is a specially marked area for passengers to get on or off buses and trolleys. You can **never** drive through a safety zone.

There is only one time when you can drive on a sidewalk. You can drive across a sidewalk only to enter or exit a driveway or alley.

The test will usually have a question about a blind pedestrian. The question will say that the person is blind, or it will say that he or she has a white cane or guide dog. If the test says anything about a white cane or guide dog, this means that the person is blind. You need to know the following three rules about blind pedestrians:

1. You always need to yield the right-of-way to a blind pedestrian.

2. If you see a blind pedestrian, you should pull up to the crosswalk so that the person can hear your car's engine.

3. If the blind pedestrian starts to cross, but then goes back onto the curb, you should stop. But if the person is waiting on the curb, you can proceed, since he or she is not ready to cross the street.

16-1. If the driver ahead of you stops at a crosswalk, what should you do? **Stop, and then proceed when all of the pedestrians have crossed.**

16-2. When may you drive across a sidewalk? **To enter or exit a driveway or alley.**

16-3. A safety zone is a specially marked area for passengers to get on or off buses or trolleys. When may you drive through a safety zone? **Never.**

16-4. Who has the right-of-way at an intersection with no crosswalks? **Pedestrians always have the right-of-way.**

16-5. There is no crosswalk and you see a pedestrian crossing your lane ahead. What should you do? **Stop and let him or her finish crossing the street.**

16-6. If you see a pedestrian with guide dog or white cane waiting to cross at a corner, what should you do? **Pull up to the crosswalk so the person can hear your engine.**

16-7. When do you need to yield the right-of-way to a pedestrian with a white cane or guide dog? **Always.**

16-8. You are making a right turn at a corner. A pedestrian with a guide dog is at the corner ready to cross the street in front of you. What should you do before you make the right turn? **Wait until the pedestrian crosses the street.**

16-9. You are waiting to turn right at a red light. There is a pedestrian waiting to cross the street you want to enter. Who has the right-of-way when the light turns green? **The pedestrian.**

16-10. Pedestrians who are blind or is visually impaired use traffic sounds before deciding to cross the street. If you see a pedestrian with a guide dog or white cane waiting to cross at a corner, what should you do? **Pull up to the crosswalk so the person can hear your engine.**

16-11. When approaching a crosswalk where a blind pedestrian is waiting to cross, what must you do? **Stop at the crosswalk and wait for the pedestrian to cross the street.**

16-12. A pedestrian starts to cross the street after the "Don't Walk" signal starts to flash, and they are still in the street when your signal changes to green. What should you do? **Wait until the pedestrian crosses the street before proceeding.**

16-13. Who has the right-of-way if a pedestrian is in a crosswalk in the middle of a block? **The pedestrian.**

16-14. Who has the right-of-way at an intersection with no crosswalks? **Pedestrians always have the right-of-way.**

16-15. You see a pedestrian with a white cane at the corner ready to cross the street. The person takes a step back and pulls in his cane. What should you do? **Stop and then proceed through the intersection, because the person is not ready to cross.**

16-16. If a pedestrian is crossing at a corner, but the crosswalk is not marked, who has the right-of-way? **The pedestrian.**

17: SPEEDING

There is almost always one question on the test about the California **"basic speed law"**. Under that law, you should never drive faster than is safe for the current road or weather conditions. In other words, if the posted speed limit is 65 and it's unsafe to drive over 40, then you could get a speeding ticket if you are driving 41 or faster. The posted speed limit only applies when there are ideal driving conditions.

In a residential area, the speed limit is 25 mph, unless there are signs showing another speed limit. The speed limit in a school zone is also 25 mph whenever there are children present. The speed limit in an alley is 15 mph.

You can never drive faster than the posted speed limit, and there might be trick questions about this. For example, if the question says that the posted speed limit is 65, but all of the other traffic is driving faster, the maximum speed is still 65.

But you shouldn't always drive slower than other traffic, because you can block traffic if you drive too slowly.

And if you are going into some hazardous situation, you should always slow down. For example, if you are going around a sharp curve at the speed limit, you need to slow down. Even if you can control your own vehicle, there might be some hazard around the curve that you can't see.

17-1. If you drive 55 mph in a 55 mph zone, can you be given a speeding ticket? **Yes, if the road or weather conditions require a slower speed.**

17-2. What is California's "Basic Speed Law"? **You should never drive faster than is safe for current conditions.**

17-3. What is the maximum speed limit for ideal driving conditions? **The posted speed for the road of freeway you are using.**

17-4. Unless otherwise posted the speed limit in a residential district is _____. **25 mph.**

17-5. What is the speed limit for a school zone where children are present? **25 mph.**

17-6. You are driving on a freeway posted for 65 mph. The traffic is traveling at 70 mph. How fast may you legally drive? **No faster than 65 mph.**

17-7. Should you always drive slower than other traffic? Why? **No. You can block traffic when you drive too slowly.**

17-8. Even if you know your vehicle can maneuver a sharp curve at the legal speed limit, you should still slow down because _____. **There may be a stalled car or collision ahead that you can't see.**

18: DRIVING IN BAD CONDITIONS

Here are the 10 facts you need to know for the test about driving in adverse conditions:

1. Bridges and overpasses are the first places to freeze. Also, there can be spots of ice hidden in these places.
2. If you are driving on a slippery surface, shift to low gear before going down a hill.
3. If your car starts to skid or hydroplane, the first thing you should do is slowly ease your foot off the gas pedal, but don't use the brakes.
4. In foggy weather, you should turn on your windshield wipers and also your **low-beam** headlights.
5. Any time your visibility is limited, slow down and turn on your **low-beam** headlights. You want your headlights on so that other drivers can see you.
6. If you are **unable** to see the road, you need to pull over and wait for visibility to get better.
7. Roadways are the most slippery the **first rain after a dry spell**.
8. Avoid deep puddles, if possible.
9. If the road is wet from a heavy rain, you should increase the distance between your vehicle and the car ahead.
10. To help avoid skidding on slippery surfaces you should slow down **before** entering curves and intersections. Also, don't make fast turns and fast stops.

18-1. When driving on a slippery surface such as snow or ice, what should you do before going down a steep hill? **Shift into a low gear.**

18-2. What freezes first when wet? **Bridges.**

18-3. On freezing wet days, where are there likely to be hidden spots of ice? **Roadways on bridges and overpasses.**

18-4. What should you do if the road is wet and your car starts to skid? **Slowly ease your foot off the gas pedal.**

18-5. What should you do if you are unable to see the road ahead while driving because of heavy fog and your wipers do not help? **Pull off the road completely until visibility improves.**

18-6. It is very foggy. What should you do? **Slow down, turn on your windshield wipers, and your low-beam lights.**

18-7. On rainy, snowy, or foggy days, why should you use your headlights? **So that other drivers can see you.**

18-8. When driving in fog, you should use your _____. **Low-beam headlights.**

18-9. When are roadways the most slippery? **The first rain after a dry spell.**

18-10. It is a very windy day. You are driving, and a dust storm blows across the freeway, reducing your visibility. What should you do? **Drive more slowly and turn on your low-beam headlights.**

18-11. Why should you turn on your headlights at dawn or dusk or in rain or snow? **So that other drivers can see you.**

18-12. When driving in fog, snow, or rain, what should you use? **Your low-beam headlights.**

18-13. If there is a deep puddle in the road ahead, what should you do? **Avoid the puddle, if possible.**

18-14. What should you do if your car starts to hydroplane (lose traction because of water on the road)? **Slow down gradually and NOT use the brakes.**

18-15. What is the best advise for driving when heavy fog or dust occurs? **Try not to drive until the conditions improve.**

18-16. When should you use your headlights? **Any time you have trouble seeing others or being seen.**

18-17. What should you do if the road is wet from a heavy rain? **Increase the distance between your vehicle and the car ahead**

18-18. What should you do to help avoid skidding on slippery surfaces? **Slow down before entering curves and intersections.**

18-19. What should you do if the road is wet and your car starts to skid? **Slowly ease your foot off the gas pedal.**

18-20. When roads are slippery, what should you do? **Avoid making fast turns and fast stops.**

19: MERGING AND LANE CHANGES

There is almost always one question on the test about changing lanes or merging. The correct answer almost always includes the information that you should **look over your shoulder**. If there is a question about changing lanes, and the answer didn't say anything about looking over your shoulder, look at it very carefully, because it might be wrong!

There are actually three things you should do before changing lanes: **Signal, check your mirrors**, and **look over your shoulder**. Sometimes, the question doesn't ask about the other two things. But it almost always asks about looking over your shoulder. Sometimes, the test asks which shoulder you should look over. This is easy: If you are merging to the left, then look over your left shoulder. If you are merging to the right, then look over your right shoulder.

When you are merging into traffic, you need at least a **4-second gap**.

19-1. What are the things you should do before you change lanes?
Signal, check your mirrors, and look over your shoulder.

19-2. Before you change lanes, what should you do to be sure a lane is clear? **Glance over your shoulder into the lane you want to enter.**

19-3. What about your signals? **You must always signal for lane changes.**

19-4. When you change lanes or merge with another lane, there needs to be _____. **At least a 4-second gap in traffic.**

19-5. If you move into the right lane, you should look over your _____ first. If you move into the left lane, you should look over your _____ first. **Right shoulder, left shoulder.**

20: PASSING

There are a few questions on the test about passing other cars, and about being passed.

Here are the two most important rules: First, to pass safely, you always need to wait for a large enough gap in the oncoming traffic. Second, you should never assume that the car you are passing will make space to let you back into your lane. It is safe to return to your lane when you can see the other car's headlights in your rearview mirror.

Never pass another vehicle if someone is likely to enter or cross the road.

If another car is turning left, it is legal to pass them on the right, but only if there is enough room on the right. You are **never** allowed to drive off the road to pass another vehicle.

Finally, if **five or more** vehicles are following you and are not able to pass, you are required to pull off the road when it is safe so that they can pass.

20-1. When are you allowed to drive off the road to pass another vehicle? **Never.**

20-2. You are driving 55 mph on a two-lane highway with one lane in each direction. You want to pass the car ahead of you. What do you need to pass safely? To pass safely? **A large enough gap in the oncoming traffic.**

20-3. What do you need to do if five or more vehicles are following you on a narrow two-lane road? **Pull off the road when it is safe and let them pass.**

20-4. When may you drive off of the paved roadway to pass another vehicle? Never.

20-5. If you plan to pass another vehicle, what should you **not** assume? **That the other driver will make space for you to return to your lane.**

20-6. There are five vehicles following closely behind you on a road with one lane in your direction. What should you do when you see this white sign?

Drive to the side of the road into the designated area.

20-7. You are on a two-way road and the vehicle ahead of you is turning left into a driveway. When may you legally pass on the right? **If there is enough road between the curb and the vehicle.**

20-8 When should you not pass another vehicle? **When someone is likely to enter or cross the road.**

20-9 When passing another vehicle, when is it safe to return to your lane? **When you can see that vehicle's headlights in your rearview mirror.**

21: FREEWAY DRIVING

The test will have one or two questions about freeway driving. Most of those topics have been covered in other chapters, but there are a few more items you should know for the test.

Slower traffic should drive in the right lanes, and faster traffic should drive in the left lanes. For example, the test sometimes shows this sign and asks what it means.

This is not a trick question, because the sign means exactly what it says. The correct answer for this question is that you should stay in the right lane if you are driving slower than other traffic. But you should also remember that this is the rule on a freeway even without this sign. So if the test asks which lane you should be in if driving slower than other cars, the answer is the right lane. This is especially true if a lot of other drivers are passing you on the right. If they are passing you on the right, that means that you are the "slower traffic", and you should be driving in the right lane. If you drive too slowly in the left lane, this can frustrate other drivers and make them angry. In fact, if most of the traffic is driving faster than you, and you are driving in the left lane, you can get a citation for obstructing the flow of traffic.

If you are driving in the right lane, you need to remember that this is the lane that other traffic will be merging into as they enter the freeway. So you need to keep your eye open for these merging vehicles. If possible, you should make room for merging traffic. This sign means that there is a merging lane ahead:

In order to see potential hazards on a freeway, always keep watching further down the road than you would on a city street.

On a freeway, a broken right line is used to mark an exit lane. One question asks what it means if you are in the right lane and you see this lane to the left of your car. It means that you are in the exit lane.

In another chapter, we talked about carpool lanes. They are usually found on freeways, so it's a good idea to review that subject. To use a carpool lane, your car needs to have the minimum number of **people** shown on the sign. Remember, the only requirement is that they be humans. There is no minimum age. So don't be confused if one of the answers tells whether they are adults or children. The only important thing is the number of people, not their ages. Therefore, one adult and two children are allowed in a 3-person carpool lane. And don't be confused by animals. You never count animals. Therefore, a car with one human and two dogs is not allowed in the carpool lane.

When you merge onto a freeway, you should be driving about the same speed as the freeway traffic. However, the test sometimes asks what to do if the traffic is not letting you in. The correct answer to this question is that you would stop at the end of the entrance ramp and wait. It's not a good idea to stop there, and you should always avoid it if possible. But if there is no gap in traffic, that's what you need to do, and that is the correct answer to this question.

One question asks what to do if you are in the left lane and need to exit from the right lane. The correct answer is that you change lanes **one lane at a time**.

On a freeway, you should generally signal lane changes for at least five seconds.

One question asks what you should do if you exit a freeway on a ramp that curves downhill. It doesn't really matter that this is on the freeway. You should do what you always do before a curve, and that is slow down to a safe speed before the curve.

21-1. What does this sign mean?

You should stay in the right lane if you are driving slower than the other traffic.

21-2. What should you do if you exit a freeway on a ramp that curves downhill? **Slow to a safe speed before the curve.**

21-3. What should you do if other drivers are not making room for you to merge onto a freeway with heavy traffic? **If necessary, you may stop before merging with the freeway traffic.**

21-4. How long should you signal on a freeway? **At least five seconds.**

21-5. You are driving in the left lane and many cars are passing you on the right. What should you do if the driver behind you wants to drive faster? **Move over to the right lane when it is safe.**

21-6. What should you do differently on a freeway from what you would do on a city street? **Look further ahead in order to see potential hazards early.**

21-7. What can happen if you drive slowly in front of traffic in the far left (fast) lane on a freeway? **It can frustrate other drivers and make them angry.**

21-8. What should you expect when driving in the far right lane of a freeway? **Merging vehicles at on-ramps.**

21-9. How fast should you be driving when merging onto a freeway? **At or near the same speed as the freeway traffic.**

21-10. What should you do if you are on the freeway and traffic is merging into your lane? **Make room for merging traffic, if possible.**

21-11. You are driving in the far right lane of a four-lane freeway and notice thick broken white lines on the left side of your lane. What does this mean? **You are driving in an exit lane.**

21-12. When can you can legally drive in a freeway carpool lane? **Only if you are carrying the minimum number of persons shown on the sign.**

21-13. You are driving on a five-lane freeway in the lane closest to the center divider. What should you do to exit the freeway on the right? **Change lanes one at a time until you are in the proper lane.**

21-14. What does this sign mean?

There is a merging lane ahead.

21-15. What could happen if you are driving 55 mph in the far left (fast) land and the speed limit is 65 mph? **You could be cited for driving too slowly, if you block the normal and reasonable flow of traffic.**

21-16. How fast should you be driving when merging onto a freeway? **At or near the same speed as the freeway traffic.**

22: ACCIDENTS AND EMERGENCIES

There are a few questions about what to do if you are involved in an accident or other emergency.

First of all, you need to have proof of insurance in the car with you. You need to show this to law enforcement if you are involved in an accident or stopped for a citation.

If you are in a collision, you need to file a written report with the DMV within 10 days. The form you need to file is called the **SR-1**. You need to do this if the property damage is over **$750**, or if there are any **injuries**.

In any accident, you are always required to give information to the other people in the accident. You must give them four things: your **driver's license information, proof of insurance, vehicle registration, and current address.**

If it is a minor accident with no injuries and only a little bit of damage, you should move your vehicle out of the traffic lane if possible.

You must show proof of insurance to law enforcement if you are involved in an accident or stopped for a citation.

If you are in an accident with a parked car and can't find the owner, you need to do two things. First of all, you need to **leave a note** on the car. You also need to **notify the police**. Normally, this would be the city police, but if it's an unincorporated area, it would be the California Highway Patrol.

If you see an accident ahead, one way to warn other drivers is to flash your brake lights and/or turn on your emergency flashers. If your car breaks down on the highway, you should always turn on your emergency flashers.

22-1. If you are involved in an accident, what do you need to exchange with the other persons involved? **Licence Information, proof of insurance, vehicle registration, and current address.**

22-2. If you are involved in a minor collision at an intersection, and there are no injuries and very little damage, what should you do? **Move your vehicle out of the traffic lane if possible.**

22-3. You must make a written report of traffic accident (SR-1) to the DMV if you are involved in a collision with more than _____ in damages. **$750.**

22-4. Even if there is not that much damage, you must notify law enforcement and make the written report (SR-1) to the DMV if _____. **There is an injury or death.**

22-5. What can you do to warn other drivers of an accident ahead? **Flash your brake lights or turn on your emergency flashers.**

22-6. What do you need to do if you have been involved in a minor traffic collision with a parked vehicle and you can't find the owner? **Leave a note on the vehicle and report the accident to city police or CHP.**

22-7. What should you do if you car has broken down on the highway? **Turn on your emergency flashers.**

23: KIDS AND SCHOOL BUSES

The test will always have one question about stopping for school buses, and/or leaving kids in a car alone.

If a **school bus is stopped with the red lights flashing**, then you need to stop and stay stopped as long as the lights are flashing.

It is always illegal to leave children **six years old or younger** unattended in a car. Sometimes, the test will add additional information. For example, it might ask if it's OK to leave them on a hot day, or leave them if the keys are in the ignition. If you get one of these questions, then the answer is that it is not OK. But be careful when you see these questions, because it is **always** illegal to leave them unattended. So if the test asks you if it is OK to leave them if you take the keys, it is still illegal. The person supervising the children needs to be at least 12 years old. So if the test asks whether it's OK to leave an eleven year old and a five year old, this is not OK. But if it asks whether it's OK to leave a five year old and a 12 year old, this would be OK.

Children under the age of one are not allowed to ride in the front seat if the car has airbags.

Finally, you must always obey instructions from school crossing guards.

23-1. A school bus ahead of you in your lane is stopped with red lights flashing. What should you do? **Stop as long as the red lights are flashing.**

23-2. Is it legal to leave children six or younger unattended in a car on a hot day, if they are secured in a child passenger restraint system? **No, it is illegal.**

23-3. When do you need to obey instructions from school crossing guards? **At all times.**

23-4. Children under the age of one should not ride in the _____ if the car is equipped with _____. **Front seat, airbags.**

23-5. When is it is legal to leave a child six years of age or younger unattended in a motor vehicle? **Only if the child is supervised by a person 12 years or older.**

23-6. True or false: It is legal to leave a child six years of a ge or younger unattended in a motor vechile if the keys are not in the ignition. **False.**

24: NEW LAWS

When new laws are passed, they are sometimes included on the test a few months later. The following questions have not yet been used, but it is possible that one of these will be added to the test before you take it. Therefore, you should also be familiar with these new laws:

If you need to show your proof of insurance (proof of financial responsibility) to a police officer, it is now legal to show an electronic version using a mobile electronic device.

If you are over 18, it is now legal to send or receive text-based communications, but only if it is voice-operated hands-free operation.

In most cases, a urine test is no longer an option to measure blood alcohol content. Therefore, most tests will now be either breath or blood.

Some hybrid and low emission vehicles are now allowed to use High Occupancy Vehicle Lanes.

It's illegal to sell or use a visual or electronic product that obscures your license plates.

24-1. If a peace officer requests it, you must show proof of financial responsibility. You may show either a _____ or _____ version. **Paper or**

electronic.

24-2. When is it legal to send or receive text-based communication while driving? **If you are over 18 and it is voice-operated hands-free operation.**

24-3. You may use a High Occupancy Vehicle lane if you have the required number of passengers or are driving a qualifying _____ vehicle. **Hybrid or low emission.**

24-4. It is illegal to sell or use visual or electronic products that obscure your _____. **License plates.**

25: MEMORIZATION

Most of the material in the previous chapters is common sense. In fact, even if you don't study for the test, you can figure out a lot of the questions by using the process of elimination and what you already know about driving.

However, there are a certain number of things that need to be memorized. Some of these will not make you a safer driver, but they will be on the test. My personal favorite is the question about dumping or abandoning an animal on the highway. I doubt it very much if you plan on dumping Fido or Fluffy by the side of the road. You would never even think of doing such a heartless thing. Therefore, there's really no reason for you to know how long you would go to jail. But Sacramento wants to make sure you know that you'll be fined $1000 and go to jail for six months. So they put it on the test, and now you know.

Here are the facts that you need to memorize for the test. I recommend that you copy or print these pages. Cover up the answers below, and make sure that you have the answer memorized. Or have a friend read all of the questions, and make sure that you can give all of the answers. If you are reading this book on an electronic device, these items are repeated below without the answers. Write down all of the answers, and then come back and make sure you have all of them right. Do this again right before the test, and make sure that you have all of these facts memorized.

Following distance from car in front	3 seconds
How far ahead of you to watch	10-15 seconds
Gap when merging	4 seconds
Signal on freeway	5 seconds
Minimum safe distance from air bags	10 inches
Age for child passenger restraint	Under 6
But passenger restraint not required if they are	over 60 pounds
Can't leave unattended in car	6 years old or younger
Old enough to stay with younger kids	12 years old or older
Over 21 illegal BAC	0.08% or higher
Under 21 illegal BAC	0.01% or higher
Penalty for not stopping for officer	1 year jail
Penalty for running from police and someone injured	7 years prison
Drunk driving penalty	6 months in jail
Penalty for dumping or abandoning animal on highway	$1000 and 6 months jail
Dim lights for oncoming vehicle	500 feet
Dim lights for vehicle in front of you	300 feet

Maximum distance in bike lane	200 feet before right turn
How to turn head at intersection	left, right, left again
Distance from curb when parallel parked	18 inches
Need to mark cargo sticking over bumper more than	4 feet
Passenegers or mail only	white curb
Park for limited time	green curb
Passengers or freight only	yellow curb
No stopping, standing, parking	red curb
Disabled parking only	blue curb
Residential speed limit	25 mph
School zone with children present	25 mph
Speed limit for alley	15 mph
Speed limit for towing trailer	55 mph
Speed limit at railroad crossing where you can't see clearly	15 mph
Speed limit at uncontrolled intersection where you can't see cross traffic	15 mph
Pull over to let them pass if this number of cars behind you	5 or more
Two times when SR1 report must be filed	$750 or injuries

Time to file SR1 report	10 days
Illegal to transport animals in truck	If not properly secured
Class C license	legal to drive 3-axle vehicle if under 6000 pounds
Selling or transferring vehicle	Notify DMV in 5 days
For 12 months after you get your license, no transporting minors without your parent or guardian during these hours	11 PM - 5 AM

Use the following pages to review all of the information you need to memorize:

Following distance from car in front

How far ahead of you to watch

Gap when merging

Signal on freeway

Minimum safe distance from air bags

Age for child passenger restraint

But passenger restraint not required if they are

Can't leave unattended in car

Old enough to stay with younger kids

Over 21 illegal BAC

Under 21 illegal BAC

Penalty for not stopping for officer

Penalty for running from police and someone injured

Drunk driving penalty

Penalty for dumping or abandoning animal on highway

Dim lights for oncoming vehicle

Dim lights for vehicle in front of you

Maximum distance in bike lane

How to turn head at intersection

Distance from curb when parallel parked

Need to mark cargo sticking over bumper more than

Passenegers or mail only

Park for limited time

Passengers or freight only

No stopping, standing, parking

Disabled parking only

Residential speed limit

School zone with children present

Speed limit for alley

Speed limit for towing trailer

Speed limit at railroad crossing where you can't see clearly

Speed limit at uncontrolled intersection where you can't see cross traffic

Pull over to let them pass if this number of cars behind you

Two times when SR1 report must be filed

Time to file SR1 report

Illegal to transport animals in truck

Class C license

Selling or transferring vehicle

For 12 months after you get your license, no transporting minors without your parent or guardian during these hours

25-1. If an uncontrolled railroad crossing is ahead and you can't see clearly if any trains are coming, what is the speed limit? **15 mph.**

25-2. At an uncontrolled intersection where you can't see cross traffic until right before the intersection, what is the speed limit? **15 mph.**

25-3. You can be fined up to $1000 and jailed for six months if you are cited for this. **Dumping or abandoning an animal on a highway.**

25-4, If a five-year-old child weighs 55 pounds, is a child passenger restraint system required? **Yes, because he or she is under 60 pounds.**

25-5. What is the speed limit if you are approaching a railroad crossing with no warning devices and are unable to see 400 feet down the tracks in one direction? **15 mph.**

25-6. When parking your vehicle parallel to the curb on a level street, how close must your wheels be to the curb? **Within 18 inches.**

25-7. It is illegal for a person 21 years of age or older to drive with a blood alcohol concentration (BAC) that is _____. **0.08% (eight hundredths of one percent) or higher.**

25-8. When can you can transport animals on the back of a pickup truck? **Only if the animals are properly secured.**

25-9. Unless otherwise posted the speed limit in a residential district is _____. **25 mph.**

25-10. With a Class C drivers license a person may drive _____. **A 3-axle vehicle if the Gross Vehicle Weight is less than 6,000 pounds.**

25-11. You must notify the DMV within 5 days if you _____. **Sell or transfer your vehicle.**

25-12. When you change lanes or merge, you need _____. **At least 4-second gap in traffic.**

25-13. You must mark cargo with a red flag or lights if it is _____. **Extending more than 4 feet from your rear bumper.**

25-14. The speed limit in any alley is ____. **15mph.**

25-15. A peace office is signaling you to drive to the edge of the roadway, but you ignore his warning and flee. You can be _____. **Jailed in the county jail for not more than 1 year.**

25-16. The speed limit for a school zone where children are present is ____. **25 mph.**

25-17. For the first 12 months after you are licensed, you must be accompanied by your parent or guardian if you transport minors between the hours of _____. **11 PM and 5AM.**

26: PRACTICE TEST

After you have read the rest of this book and memorized the information in chapter 25, you are ready to take this practice test. This test is the same as the questions at the end of each chapter, but without the answers. The correct answers are given at the end.

This practice test is harder than the actual test because it is "fill in the blank", and you need to come up with the right answer. The actual test will be easier because it is multiple choice. Since you will know the correct answer, you will be able to spot it right away.

Many of these questions have more than one correct answer. Therefore, don't be worried if you come up with another correct answer at first. But you should try to give the answer shown here, because that is the one that will probably be on the test.

There are two ways that you can take this test. If you want to write down the answers, then use the questions here, and then compare your answers to the ones at the end. Or, you can have a friend read the questions and you give the answers. If you do it that way, it will be easier to use the questions at the end of each chapter, since your friend can tell you right away if you have the right answer. Either way, keep track of the questions you get wrong, and go back and study that chapter.

When you have finished this test, then go to the DMV website and take the practice tests there. You should get all of the questions right at that point. If you get one or two wrong, re-read that section of the Driver Handbook, and make sure you understand why you got it wrong.

Finally, right before you take the test, go through the information in chapter 25, and make sure that you have it all memorized.

1-1.The "_____-second rule" applies to the space in front of your vehicle.

1-2. What should you do to see how traffic is moving behind you?

1-3. To see potential hazards early, what should you do?

1- 4. When is backing up a vehicle dangerous?

1-5. What should you do if it will prevent an accident?

1-6. When do collisions tend to happen?

1-7. You will probably interfere with the flow of traffic and get a ticket if

1-8. You see a car approaching from the rear. When you check your mirror again to change lanes, you can't see that car. What should you do?

1-9. What should you do if a driver looks like he or she is going to pull out in front of you?

1-10. What will happen if you drive faster than other vehicles on a road with one lane in each direction and continually pass the other cars?

1-11. At intersections, crosswalks, and railroad crossings, you should always:

1-12. You drive defensively when you _____.

1-13. What can happen when you tailgate other drivers (drive close to their rear bumper)?

1-14. Why should you have a "space cushion" around your vehicle?

1-15. What should you do when you are near schools, playgrounds, or residential areas?

1- 16. What should you do if there is one lane in your direction and the vehicle ahead of you often slows down for no apparent reason?

1-17. It helps to improve traffic flow if you do this at an accident scene:

1-18. You are driving, and there are oncoming cars on your left and a row of parked cars on your right. Where should you steer?

1-19. Three of the most important times to check traffic behind you are before:

1-20. What should you do if you approach a curve or the top of a hill and you do not have a clear view of the road ahead?

1-21. If you are being tailgated by another driver what should you do?

1-22. When should you should use your horn?

1-23. What are things you should do to safely back up?

1-24. Do you need to tap your horn before you back up?

1-25. What should you do if another car suddenly cuts in front of you can creates a hazard?

1-26. Why shouldn't you slow down just to look at accidents or other unusual things?

1-27. What should you do to see how traffic is moving behind you?

1-28. You are approaching a sharp curve in the road. What should you do?

1-29. When should you should adjust your rear view and side view mirrors?

1-30. Why is it dangerous to drive along the right-rear side of another vehicle?

1-31. Where should you drive on a multilane street with two way traffic?

1-32. What should you never assume about other drivers?

1-33. On a sharp curve, when should you use your brakes to slow your vehicle?

1-34. What do you need to do to see vehicles in your blind spots?

1-35. What should you do if you see a car approaching from the rear, but when you check your mirror to change lanes, you no longer see the car?

1-36. Why shouldn't you tailgate (follow closely behind another vehicle)?

1-37. What should you do if you are approaching a sharp curve in the road?

1-38. What are the three most important times to check traffic behind you?

1-39. What should you do if you approach a curve or the top of a hill and you do not have a clear view of the road ahead?

1-40. What do you need to do to see vehicles in your blind spots?

1-41. What should you do if you are being tailgated by another driver?

1-42. What should you do if you see a vehicle stopped on the right shoulder of the road ahead with its hazard lights on?

2-1. If you are riding in a vehicle with a lap belt and also a separate shoulder belt what are you required to do?

2-2. When are you are required to use your seat belt?

2-3. If you don't wear your safety belt in a moving vehicle, what will happen?

2-4. If a passenger is younger than 16 and is not wearing a seat belt, what will happen?

2-5. If your car has air bags, where are you safest?

2-6. What is true about safety belts and collisions?

2-7. All children under age six riding in your vehicle must use a child passenger restraint system unless:

2-8. The only time you can legally ride in the back of a pickup truck is:

3-1. You are being chased by a police vehicle with its light and sirens activated. You ignore the warning to stop and speed away. During the chase, a person is seriously injured. What is the penalty?

3-2. What should you do if you see an emergency vehicle with flashing lights behind you?

3-3. What should you do if you are crossing an intersection and an emergency vehicle is approaching with a siren and flashing lights?

4-1. The safest precaution that you can take regarding the use of cell phones when driving is:

4-2. It is illegal and dangerous to do what while driving.

4-3. When is it legal to use a cell phone without a hands-free device while driving?

4-4. What should you do if your cell phone rings while you are driving and you do not have a hands-free device?

5-1. If there is a double solid yellow line dividing opposite lanes of traffic, when may you cross the lines?

5-2. When can you cross two sets of solid, double, yellow lines that are two or more feet apart?

5-3. When may you may cross a double, yellow line to pass another vehicle?

5-4. A solid yellow line next to a broken yellow line means that vehicles next to the broken line may do what?

5-5. You are not allowed to cross double solid yellow lines in the center of the roadway to ___.

5-6. Two sets of solid double yellow lines (more than two feet apart) should be treated the same as what?

5-7. If there are two solid yellow lines in the center of the road, are you allowed to cross the lines to turn left into a driveway?

5-8. What do solid yellow lines separate?

5-9. What do yellow lines separate?

6-1. Using low beams during the day on narrow country roads is:

6-2. You are driving at night on a dimly lit street and using high beams. You should dim your lights when you are within _____ of an oncoming vehicle.

6-3. When driving in traffic at night on a dimly lit street, you should drive slowly enough so that _____.

6-4. You are driving at night on a dimly lit street and using high beams. You should dim your lights when you are within _____ of a vehicle you are approaching from behind.

6-5. If an oncoming vehicle fails to dim its high beams, what should you do?

6-6. At night, when should you use your high-beam headlights?

6-7. When are you allowed to drive using only your parking lights?

7-1. If you are towing another vehicle or trailer on a freeway with four lanes in your direction, where may you may travel?

7- 2. What should you do if you are following a large tour bus?

7-3. If you want to pass a bicyclist riding on the right edge of your lane, what should you do?

7-4. You want to pass a bicyclist in a narrow traffic lane, and an oncoming car is approaching. What should you do?

7-5. If you want to turn right and your driving lane is next to a bicycle lane, what should you do?

7-6. You are driving on the freeway. The vehicle in front of you is a large truck. Where should you drive?

7-7. Why do you need more space in front of your vehicle when following a large truck?

7-8. When can you drive in a bike lane?

7-9. What is true about the apparent speed of large trucks?

7-10. Large trucks take _____ than passenger cars.

7-11. What is true about motorcyclists and motorists?

7-12. If a vehicle is displaying a diamond-shaped sign, then it must _____.

7-13. What is true about blind spots in trucks?

7-14. Why do large trucks often travel with a lot of space in front of them?

7-15. What kind of vehicle must always stop before crossing railroad tracks?

7-16. A large truck is ahead of you and is turning right onto a street with two lanes in each direction. What might happen?

7-17. If a truck is turning right, what might happen?

7-18. When might a large truck lose speed and cause a hazard?

7-19. Why must you carefully watch for bicycles in traffic lanes?

7-20. Why can bicycles sometimes use the same lanes used by motor vehicles?

8-1.

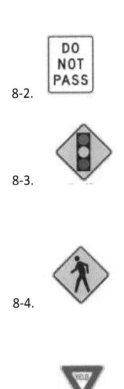

8-2.

8-3.

8-4.

8-6.

8-6.

8-7.

8-8.

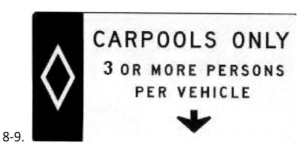

8-9.

Which example is given on the test of a car that's allowed to use this lane?

8-10.

8-11.

8-12.

8-13.

8-14.

8-16.   What does this sign mean on a vehicle:

8-16.

8-17.

8-18.

8-21.

8-22.

9-1. You see a signal person at a road construction site ahead. What do you need to do?

9-2. In a construction zone, who is responsible for the safety of the road workers?

9-3. What should you do when you are driving near construction zones?

9-4. At a construction site, you are always required to obey Instructions from _____.

9-5. When driving near road construction zones, what should you do?

9-6. _____-colored road signs warn you of road workers or road equipment ahead.

10-1. What should you do when a light turns yellow?

10-2. When approaching an intersection at the posted speed limit when the signal light turns yellow, what should you do?

10-3. If you are going to make a left turn from the left-turn lane and the yellow arrow appears, what should you do?

10-4. Where should you stop your vehicle if there is no crosswalk or limit line?

10-5. If a police officer signals you to continue driving through a red light, what should you do?

10-6. You are approaching an intersection at the posted speed limit when the signal light turns yellow. What should you do

10-7. Is it legal to block an intersection during rush hour if you have the green light?

10-8. When can you legally turn right on a solid red light?

10-9. For which traffic lights must you always stop your vehicle?

10-10. On a traffic light, what does it mean if a red arrow is pointing to the right?

10-11. What should you do if a traffic signal light isn't working at an intersection?

10-12. What is the difference between a traffic light with a red arrow and one with a red light?

10-13. When may you legally block an intersection?

10-14. If you have a green light, but traffic is blocking the intersection, what should you do?

10-15. You see a flashing yellow traffic signal at an upcoming intersection. What does the flashing yellow light mean?

10-16. What should you do if you approach an intersection without a stop sign or signals?

10-17. You reach an intersection with stop signs on all four corners at the same time as another the driver on your left. Who has the right of way?

10-18. What does a flashing yellow traffic signal at an intersection mean?

10-19. What does a flashing red light at an intersection mean?

10-20. Two vehicles are approaching an uncontrolled "T" intersection. One vehicle is on the through road, and the other is on the road that ends. Who has the right-of-way at the intersection?

10-21. What should you do if you have a green light, but traffic is blocking the intersection?

10-22. You should never start across an intersection if you know

_____.

10-23. What should you do if you approach an intersection without a stop sign or signals?

10-24. You are stopped at an intersection, and the traffic light just turned green. Should you go immediately?

10-25. Before driving into an intersection from a stop, you should look

_____.

10-26. If you cannot stop safely at a yellow traffic light, what should you do?

10-27. What should you do if you are approaching an uncontrolled intersection?

11-1. If you are driving on a two-way street and you want to turn left at an upcoming corner, what do you need to do?

11-2. You can make a right turn at a solid red light if the following three things are true:

11-3. You are on a two-way street with two lanes in each direction. To turn left, where do you start the turn?

11-4.   You are about to make a left turn. You must signal continuously during the last ____ feet before the turn.

11-5. Why should you continuously signal while turning?

11-6. To turn left from a multilane one-way street onto a one-way street, what lane should you turn from?

11-7. You want to make a right turn at an upcoming intersection. How far ahead should you start signaling?

11-8. Using your turn signal at least ___ feet before turning can help you avoid _____.

11-9. You are getting ready to make a right turn. What should you do first?

11-10. You are driving on a one-way street. You may turn left onto another one-way street only if:

11-11. To turn left from a one way street with multiple lanes onto a two way street, where should you start the turn?

11-12. You are getting ready to make a right turn. You should _____ signal during the last ____ feet before you turn.

11-13. To turn left from a one-way street, where should you start from?

11-14. You may make a left turn on a red light only from a _____ onto _____.

11-15. To make a right turn from a two-way street onto another two-way street, you should start in the right-hand lane (the lane closest to the curb), and also end in right-hand lane (the lane closest to the curb).

11-16. It is a good habit to signal continuously during the last _____ before you turn at an intersection, even if you do not see any other vehicles around.

11-17. You are getting ready to make a right turn. You must signal during the last _____ before your turn.

11-18. When you want to turn left at an upcoming corner, you must give the right-of-way to ____.

11-19. You enter a designated turn lane to make a left turn at an upcoming intersection. There is oncoming traffic. What do you need to do?

11-20. You want to turn left ahead. In the middle of the road, there is a lane marked as shown:

Before you turn, what do you need to do?

11-21. What is the lane in the middle of a two-way street used for?

11-22. If you are making a right turn from a highway with two lanes in your direction, what lane should you turn from?

12-1. Name one legal U-turn?

12-2. Unless prohibited by a sign, where can you may legally make a U-turn?

12-3. In a business district, where can you legally make a U-turn?

12-4. You are driving on a divided street with multiple lanes in your direction. If you need to make a U-turn, where should you start?

13-1. If you want to go into a store to make a quick purchase, what should you do?

13-2. What does a curb painted blue mean?

13-3. When you park your car on any hill, what do you need to do?

13-4. When parking your vehicle parallel to the curb on a level street, your wheels must be within _____ of the curb.

13-5. When parking downhill on a two-way road with no curb, turn your front wheels _____.

13-6. What should you do if you were parked and have been waiting a long time in heavy traffic with your turn signal on to re-enter traffic?

13-7. When parking next to a curb, when should you use your turn signals?

13-8. When parking downhill next to a curb, how should you turn your front wheels?

13-9. When is parking permitted in a cross-hatched (diagonal) pattern space?

13-10. You park your car at the curb on a level two-way street. Before getting out of your car, what should you do?

13-11. A white painted curb means _____.

13-12. When parking uphill on a two-way street with no curbs, your front wheels should be _____.

13-13. When parked uphill next to a curb, your front wheels should be _____.

13-14. When may you park next to a red painted curb?

13-15. Is it legal to park your vehicle in an unmarked crosswalk?

13-16. Your wheels should be pointed straight ahead, unless you are _____.

13-17. If you enter traffic from a stop (for example, pulling away from the curb) you need _____.

13-18. Turn your front wheels toward the curb when you park _____.

14-1. When should you stop before crossing railroad tracks?

14-2. When sharing the road with a light rail vehicle, what should you never do?

14-3. What does this sign mean?

14-4. When can you legally go around or under a railroad crossing gate?

14-5. When should you stop before you cross railroad tracks ?

14-6. You must stop at the intersection ahead. Just before the intersection, you need to cross railroad tracks. What should you do?

14-7. What should you do when sharing the road with a light rail vehicle?

15-1. It is illegal to drive with a blood alcohol concentration (BAC) that is _____.

15-2. If you are driving in California, you have consented to what?

15-3. What is the most important thing to remember about drinking alcohol and driving?

15-4. Whose responsibility is it to know how your medications affect your driving?

15-5. Smoking inside a vehicle when a person younger than 18 years of age is present is_____.

15-6. If you are convicted of driving with an excessive blood alcohol concentration (BAC), you may be sentenced to _____.

15-7. Can over-the-counter drugs can impair your driving?

15-8. What can most cold medications do?

15-9. When can you should drive under the influence of any medication that impairs your driving?

15-10. When is it illegal to smoke inside a vehicle?

15-11. When is it legal to drive with an open alcoholic beverage container?

15-12. If you are under 21 years of age to drive with a blood alcohol concentration (BAC) that is _____.

16-1. If the driver ahead of you stops at a crosswalk, what should you do?

16-2. When may you drive across a sidewalk?

16-3. A safety zone is a specially marked area for passengers to get on or off buses or trolleys. When may you drive through a safety zone?

16-4. Who has the right-of-way at an intersection with no crosswalks?

16-5. There is no crosswalk and you see a pedestrian crossing your lane ahead. What should you do?

16-6. If you see a pedestrian with guide dog or white cane waiting to cross at a corner, what should you do?

16-7. When do you need to yield the right-of-way to a pedestrian with a white cane or guide dog?

16-8. You are making a right turn at a corner. A pedestrian with a guide dog is at the corner ready to cross the street in front of you. What should you do before you make the right turn?

16-9. You are waiting to turn right at a red light. There is a pedestrian waiting to cross the street you want to enter. Who has the right-of-way when the light turns green?

16-10. Pedestrians who are blind or is visually impaired use traffic sounds before deciding to cross the street. If you see a pedestrian with a guide dog or white cane waiting to cross at a corner, what should you do?

16-11. When approaching a crosswalk where a blind pedestrian is waiting to cross, what must you do?

16-12. A pedestrian starts to cross the street after the "Don't Walk" signal starts to flash, and they are still in the street when your signal changes to green. What should you do?

16-13. Who has the right-of-way if a pedestrian is in a crosswalk in the middle of a block?

16-14. Who has the right-of-way at an intersection with no crosswalks?

16-15. You see a pedestrian with a white cane at the corner ready to cross the street. The person takes a step back and pulls in his cane. What should you do? \

16-16. If a pedestrian is crossing at a corner, but the crosswalk is not marked, who has the right-of-way?

17-1. If you drive 55 mph in a 55 mph zone, can you be given a speeding ticket?

17-2. What is California's "Basic Speed Law"?

17-3. What is the maximum speed limit for ideal driving conditions?

17-4. Unless otherwise posted the speed limit in a residential district is
_____.

17-5. What is the speed limit for a school zone where children are present?

17-6. You are driving on a freeway posted for 65 mph. The traffic is traveling at 70 mph. How fast may you legally drive?

17-7. Should you always drive slower than other traffic? Why?

17-8. Even if you know your vehicle can maneuver a sharp curve at the legal speed limit, you should still slow down because _____.

18-1. When driving on a slippery surface such as snow or ice, what should you do before going down a steep hill?

18-2. What freezes first when wet?

18-3. On freezing wet days, where are there likely to be hidden spots of ice?

18-4. What should you do if the road is wet and your car starts to skid?

18-5. What should you do if you are unable to see the road ahead while driving because of heavy fog and your wipers do not help?

18-6. It is very foggy. What should you do?

18-7. On rainy, snowy, or foggy days, why should you use your headlights?

18-8. When driving in fog, you should use your _____.

18-9. When are roadways the most slippery?

18-10. It is a very windy day. You are driving, and a dust storm blows across the freeway, reducing your visibility. What should you do?

18-11. Why should you turn on your headlights at dawn or dusk or in rain or snow?

18-12. When driving in fog, snow, or rain, what should you use?

18-13. If there is a deep puddle in the road ahead, what should you do?

18-14. What should you do if your car starts to hydroplane (lose traction because of water on the road)?

18-15. What is the best advise for driving when heavy fog or dust occurs?

18-16. When should you use your headlights?

18-17. What should you do if the road is wet from a heavy rain?

18-18. What should you do to help avoid skidding on slippery surfaces?

18-19. What should you do if the road is wet and your car starts to skid?

18-20. When roads are slippery, what should you do?

19-1. What are the things you should do before you change lanes?

19-2. Before you change lanes, what should you do to be sure a lane is clear?

19-3. What about your signals?

19-4. When you change lanes or merge with another lane, there needs to be _____.

19-5. If you move into the right lane, you should look over your _____ first. If you move into the left lane, you should look over your _____ first.

20-1. When are you allowed to drive off the road to pass another vehicle?

20-2. You are driving 55 mph on a two-lane highway with one lane in each direction. You want to pass the car ahead of you. What do you need to pass safely? To pass safely?

20-3. What do you need to do if five or more vehicles are following you on a narrow two-lane road?

20-4. When may you drive off of the paved roadway to pass another vehicle?

20-5. If you plan to pass another vehicle, what should you not assume?

20-6. There are five vehicles following closely behind you on a road with one lane in your direction. What should you do when you see this white sign?

20-7. You are on a two-way road and the vehicle ahead of you is turning left into a driveway. When may you legally pass on the right?

20-8 When should you not pass another vehicle?

20-9 When passing another vehicle, when is it safe to return to your lane?

21-1. What does this sign mean?

21-2. What should you do if you exit a freeway on a ramp that curves downhill?

21-3. What should you do if other drivers are not making room for you to merge onto a freeway with heavy traffic?

21-4. How long should you signal on a freeway?

21-5. You are driving in the left lane and many cars are passing you on the right. What should you do if the driver behind you wants to drive faster?

21-6. What should you do differently on a freeway from what you would do on a city street?

21-7. What can happen if you drive slowly in front of traffic in the far left (fast) lane on a freeway?

21-8. What should you expect when driving in the far right lane of a freeway?

21-9. How fast should you be driving when merging onto a freeway?

21-10. What should you do if you are on the freeway and traffic is merging into your lane?

21-11. You are driving in the far right lane of a four-lane freeway and notice thick broken white lines on the left side of your lane. What does this mean?

21-12. When can you can legally drive in a freeway carpool lane?

21-13. You are driving on a five-lane freeway in the lane closest to the center divider. What should you do to exit the freeway on the right?

21-14. What does this sign mean?

21-15. What could happen if you are driving 55 mph in the far left (fast) land and the speed limit is 65 mph?

21-16. How fast should you be driving when merging onto a freeway?

22-1. If you are involved in an accident, what do you need to exchange with the other persons involved?

22-2. If you are involved in a minor collision at an intersection, and there are no injuries and very little damage, what should you do?

22-3. You must make a written report of traffic accident (SR-1) to the DMV if you are involved in a collision with more than _____ in damages.

22-4. Even if there is not that much damage, you must notify law enforcement and make the written report (SR-1) to the DMV if

_____.

22-5. What can you do to warn other drivers of an accident ahead?

22-6. What do you need to do if you have been involved in a minor traffic collision with a parked vehicle and you can't find the owner?

22-7. What should you do if you car has broken down on the highway?

23-1. A school bus ahead of you in your lane is stopped with red lights flashing. What should you do?

23-2. Is it legal to leave children six or younger unattended in a car on a hot day, if they are secured in a child passenger restraint system?

23-3. When do you need to obey instructions from school crossing guards?

23-4. Children under the age of one should not ride in the _____ if the car is equipped with _____.

23-5. When is it is legal to leave a child six years of age or younger unattended in a motor vehicle?

23-6. True or false: It is legal to leave a child six years of a ge or younger unattended in a motor vechile if the keys are not in the ignition.

24-1. If a peace officer requests it, you must show proof of financial responsibility. You may show either a _____ or _____ version.

24-2. When is it legal to send or receive text-based communication while driving?

24-3. You may use a High Occupancy Vehicle lane if you have the required number of passengers or are driving a qualifying _____ vehicle.

24-4. It is illegal to sell or use visual or electronic products that obscure your _____.

25-1. If an uncontrolled railroad crossing is ahead and you can't see clearly if any trains are coming, what is the speed limit?

25-2. At an uncontrolled intersection where you can't see cross traffic until right before the intersection, what is the speed limit?

25-3. You can be fined up to $1000 and jailed for six months if you are cited for this.

25-4, If a five-year-old child weighs 55 pounds, is a child passenger restraint system required?

25-5. What is the speed limit if you are approaching a railroad crossing with no warning devices and are unable to see 400 feet down the tracks in one direction?

25-6. When parking your vehicle parallel to the curb on a level street, how close must your wheels be to the curb?

25-7. It is illegal for a person 21 years of age or older to drive with a blood alcohol concentration (BAC) that is _____.

25-8. When can you can transport animals on the back of a pickup truck?

25-9. Unless otherwise posted the speed limit in a residential district is ____.

25-10. With a Class C drivers license a person may drive _____.

25-11. You must notify the DMV within 5 days if you _____.

25-12. When you change lanes or merge, you need _____.

25-13. You must mark cargo with a red flag or lights if it is _____.

25-14. The speed limit in any alley is ____.

25-15. A peace office is signaling you to drive to the edge of the roadway, but you ignore his warning and flee. You can be _____.

25-16. The speed limit for a school zone where children are present is ____.

25-17. For the first 12 months after you are licensed, you must be accompanied by your parent or guardian if you transport minors between the hours of _____.

Answers to Practice Questions

1-1.   Three

1-2. Check your mirrors often.

1-3. Look 10-15 seconds ahead of you.

1-4. Always.

1-5. Yield your legal right-of-way.

1-6. When one vehicle is traveling faster or slower than the flow of traffic.

1-7. You drive slower than the flow of traffic.

1-8. Look over your shoulder to make sure the car isn't in your blind spot.

1-9. Slow or stop your car and use your horn.

1-10. You will increase your chances of an accident.

1-11. Look to the sides of your vehicle to see what is coming.

1-12. Keep your eyes moving to look for possible hazards.

1-13. You can frustrate the other drivers and make them angry.

1-14. To give time to react if another driver makes a mistake.

1-15. Drive more carefully.

1- 16. Increase the following distance between you and other vehicle.

1-17.   Not slow down to look.

1-18. A middle course between the oncoming and parked cars.

1-19. Backing, changing lanes, or slowing down quickly.

1-20. Slow down so you can stop if necessary.

1-21. Increase the distance between your car and the one in front of you.

1-22. When it may help prevent an accident.

1-23. Check behind your vehicle before you get in, and look over your right shoulder as you back up.

1-24. No.

1-25. Take your foot off the gas.

1-26. It causes traffic congestion.

1-27. Check your mirrors often.

1-28. Start braking before you enter the curve.

1-29. Before you start driving

1-30. Because you're probably in one of the driver's blind spots.

1-31. Ahead of or behind the other vehicles.

1-32. Never assume that they will give you the right-of-way.

1-33. Before you enter the curve.

1-34. Look over your shoulders.

1-35. Look over your shoulder to be sure the car isn't in your blind spot:

1-36. Because it is a common cause of rear-end collisions.

1-37. Start braking before you enter the curve.

1-38. When you are backing, changing lanes, or slowing down quickly.

1-39. Slow down so you can stop if necessary.

1-40. Turn your head.

1-41. Increase the distance between your car and the vehicle ahead.

1-42. Slow down and pass very carefully.

2-1. Use both the lap belt and shoulder belt.

2-2. Whenever you are in a vehicle that is equipped with seat belts.

2-3. You will receive a traffic ticket.

2-4. The driver can receive a citation.

2-5. At least 10 inches away from the steering wheel.

2-6. Safety belts increase your chances of survival in most types of collisions.

2-7. They weigh 60 pounds or more and wear a safety belt.

2-8. If you are secured in a seat and using an approved safety belt.

3-1. Imprisonment in a state prison for up to seven years

3-2. Drive as near to the right edge of the road as possible and stop.

3-3. Continue through the intersection, pull to the right, and stop

4-1. Use hands-free devices so you can keep both hands on the steering wheel.

4-2. Listen to music through headphones that cover both ears.

4-3. Only when making a call for emergency assistance.

4-4. Let the call go to voicemail.

5-1. To make a left turn from or into a side street.

5-2. Never. You may not cross them for any reason.

5-3. If the yellow line next to your side of the road is a broken line.

5-4. Pass other vehicles.

5-5. Pass other vehicles.

5-6. A solid wall and never crossed.

5-7. Yes.

5-8. Vehicles traveling in opposite directions.

5-9. Traffic moving in opposite directions on a two-way road.

6-1. A proper use of your vehicle lights.

6-2. 500 feet.

6-3. You can stop within the area lighted by your headlights.

6-4. 300 feet.

6-5. Look toward the right edge of your lane.

6-6. Whenever it is legal and safe.

6-7. Never.

7-1. Either of the two right lanes.

7- 2. Allow extra space in front of your vehicle.

7-3. Allow a minimum of 3 feet between you and the cyclist.

7-4. Slow down and let the car pass, then pass the bicyclist.

7-5. Merge into the bicycle lane before making your turn.

7-6. Further behind the truck than you would for a passenger vehicle.

7-7. Because you need the extra room to see around the truck.

7-8. When you are within 200 feet of a cross street where you plan to turn right.

7-9. Trucks often appear to travel more slowly because of their large size.

7-10. Longer to stop.

7-11. Motorcyclists have the same rights and responsibilities as other motorists.

7-12. before crossing railroad tracks.

7-13. Large trucks have bigger blind spots than most passenger vehicles.

7-14. Because the truck driver needs to use the extra space for stopping the vehicle.

7-15. Tank trucks marked with hazardous materials placards.

7-16. The truck may have to swing wide to complete the right turn.

7-17. It might use part of the left lane to complete the turn.

7-18. Going up long or steep hills.

7-19. Because they could be hidden in your blind spots.

7-20. Because they are entitled to share the road with you.

8-1. You may not enter the road from your direction

8-2. You can't pass other vehicles for any reason.

8-3. There is a traffic signal ahead.

8-4. There is a pedestrian crosswalk ahead

8-5.   You should give the right-of-way to traffic on the road you wish to enter or cross

8-6. You must give the right-of-way to other drivers.

8-7. Another road crosses yours ahead.

8-8. You should be prepared to stop if children are in the crosswalk.

8-9. A convertible with an adult and two children.

8-10. There is a pedestrian crossing ahead.

8-11. You may not enter the road from your direction.

8-12. You may turn left on a green light when it is safe.

8-13. You are approaching a railroad crossing. Prepare to stop.

8-14. You should stop and check traffic in all directions before proceeding.

8-15. It is a slow-moving vehicle.

8-16. Look, listen, and prepare to stop at the crossing, if necessary.

8-17. The right lane will end ahead.

8-18. Vehicles on this road travel in two directions.

8-19. There is a sharp turn to the right.

8-20.   here is road work ahead.

9-1. Obey his or her instructions at all times.

9-2. You are.

9-3. Reduce speed and be prepared to stop.

9-4. Flaggers (signal persons).

9-5. Pass the construction zone carefully and avoid "rubbernecking."

9-6. Orange.

10-1. You should stop before entering the intersection, if you can do so safely.

10-2. Stop before entering the intersection, if you can do so safely

10-3. Be prepared to obey the next signal that appears.

10-4. At the corner.

10-5. Do as the officer tells you.

10-6. Stop before entering the intersection, if you can do so safely.

10-7. No.

10-8. Only after stopping, unless otherwise posted.

10-9. Solid red lights, flashing red lights, and blacked-out traffic signals.

10-10. You may not turn that direction until the light turns green.

10-11. You should come to a complete stop then proceed when it is safe.

10-12. If there is a red arrow, you are not allowed to turn, even if you stop first.

10-13. Under no circumstances.

10-14. Stay out of the intersection until traffic clears.

10-15. Slow down and cross the intersection carefully.

10-16. Slow down and be ready to stop if necessary.

10-17. You do.

10-18. Slow down and be alert at the intersection.

10-19. Stop before entering.

10-20. The vehicle on the through road.

10-21. Stay out of the intersection and wait until traffic clears.

10-22. You will block the intersection when the light turns red.

10-23. Slow down and be ready to stop if necessary.

10-24. No. You must wait until other vehicles clear the intersection before you enter.

10-25. Left, right, and left again.

10-26. Enter the intersection cautiously and continue across.

10-27. Slow down and be ready to stop.

11-1. Give the right-of-way to vehicles coming toward you.

11-2. 1. You check for pedestrians and other traffic; 2. you stop first; and 3. there is no sign to prohibit the turn.

11-3. The left lane for traffic in your direction.

11-4.   100 feet.

11-5. Because it lets other drivers know what your intentions are.

11-6. The lane closest to the left curb.

11-7. 100 feet before turning.

11-8. 100 feet, getting hit from behind.

11-9. Slow down or stop, if necessary, and then make the turn.

11-10. The traffic on that street moves to the left.

11-11. The far left lane.

11-12. Signal, 100.

11-13. The lane closest to the left curb.

11-14. One-way street, another one-way street.

11-15. Start in the right-hand lane (the lane closest to the curb), and also end in right-hand lane (the lane closest to the curb).

11-16. 100 feet.

11-17. 100 feet.

11-24. All approaching vehicles.

11-25. Signal before you arrive at the intersection.

11-23. Merge completely into that lane.

11-24. Begin or end left turns, or start a permitted U-turn.

11-25. The lane closest to the curb or the edge of the highway.

12-1. On a highway where there is a paved opening for a turn.

12-2. At an intersection with a green light.

12-3. Only at intersections, unless a sign prohibits them.

12-4. In the left lane.

13-1. Stop the engine and set the parking brake.

13-2. Parking is allowed only for disabled persons with special plates or placard.

13-3. Set your parking brake and leave your vehicle in gear or the "park" position.

13-4. 18 inches.

13-5. Right (toward the side of the road).

13-6. Continue waiting and yielding to traffic in the lane.

13-7. When pulling next to or away from the curb.

13-8. Into the curb.

13-9. Never.

13-10. Look for cars or bicycles on the traffic side of your car.

13-11. Loading zone for passengers or mail only.

13-12. Turned to the right (away from the street).

13-13. Turned away from the curb.

13-14. Never.

13-15. No.

13-16. Parked on a hill or sloping driveway.

13-17. A large enough gap to get up to the speed of traffic.

13-18. Facing downhill.

14-1. Any time a train may be approaching, whether or not you can see it.

14-2. When sharing the road with a light rail vehicle, what should you never do? Turn in front of an approaching light rail vehicle.

14-3. Look, listen, and prepare to stop at the crossing, if necessary.

14-4. Never.

14-5. You don't have room on the other side to completely cross the tracks.

14-6. Stop before the tracks if you don't have room to completely cross the tracks.

14-7. Monitor all traffic signals closely because light rail vehicles can interrupt traffic signals.

15-1. 0.08% or higher.

15-2. To take a chemical test for the alcohol content of your blood, breath, or urine if asked by a law enforcement.

15-3. Alcohol affects your judgment, which you need for driving safely.

15-4. Yours.

15-5. Illegal at all times.

15-6. Up to six months in jail.

15-7. Yes.

15-8. Make you drowsy.

15-9. Never.

15-10. Any time a person younger than 18 years of age is present is.

15-11. If it is in the trunk.

15-12. 0.01% or more.

16-1. Stop, and then proceed when all of the pedestrians have crossed.

16-2. To enter or exit a driveway or alley.

16-3. Never.

16-4. Pedestrians always have the right-of-way.

16-5. Stop and let him or her finish crossing the street.

16-6. Pull up to the crosswalk so the person can hear your engine.

16-7. Always.

16-8. Wait until the pedestrian crosses the street.

16-9. The pedestrian.

16-10. Pull up to the crosswalk so the person can hear your engine.

16-11. Stop at the crosswalk and wait for the pedestrian to cross the street.

16-12. Wait until the pedestrian crosses the street before proceeding.

16-13. The pedestrian.

16-14. Pedestrians always have the right-of-way.

16-15. Stop and then proceed through the intersection, because the person is not ready to cross.

16-16. The pedestrian.

17-1. Yes, if the road or weather conditions require a slower speed.

17-2. You should never drive faster than is safe for current conditions.

17-3. The posted speed for the road of freeway you are using.

17-4. 25 mph.

17-5. 25 mph.

17-6. No faster than 65 mph.

17-7. No. You can block traffic when you drive too slowly.

17-8. There may be a stalled car or collision ahead that you can't see.

18-1. Shift into a low gear.

18-2. Bridges.

18-3. Roadways on bridges and overpasses.

18-4. Slowly ease your foot off the gas pedal.

18-5. Pull off the road completely until visibility improves.

18-6. Slow down, turn on your windshield wipers, and your low-beam lights.

18-7. So that other drivers can see you.

18-8. Low-beam headlights.

18-9. The first rain after a dry spell.

18-10. Drive more slowly and turn on your low-beam headlights.

18-11. So that other drivers can see you.

18-12. Your low-beam headlights.

18-13. Avoid the puddle, if possible.

18-14. Slow down gradually and NOT use the brakes.

18-15. Try not to drive until the conditions improve.

18-16. Any time you have trouble seeing others or being seen.

18-17. Increase the distance between your vehicle and the car ahead

18-18. Slow down before entering curves and intersections.

18-19. Slowly ease your foot off the gas pedal.

18-20. Avoid making fast turns and fast stops.

19-1. Signal, check your mirrors, and look over your shoulder.

19-2. Glance over your shoulder into the lane you want to enter.

19-3. You must always signal for lane changes.

19-4. At least a 4-second gap in traffic.

19-5. Right shoulder, left shoulder.

20-1. Never.

20-2. A large enough gap in the oncoming traffic.

20-3. Pull off the road when it is safe and let them pass.

20-4. Never.

20-5. That the other driver will make space for you to return to your lane.

20-6. Drive to the side of the road into the designated area.

20-7. If there is enough road between the curb and the vehicle.

20-8 When someone is likely to enter or cross the road.

20-9 When you can see that vehicle's headlights in your rearview mirror.

21-1. You should stay in the right lane if you are driving slower than the other traffic.

21-2. Slow to a safe speed before the curve.

21-3. If necessary, you may stop before merging with the freeway traffic.

21-4. At least five seconds.

21-5. Move over to the right lane when it is safe.

21-6. Look further ahead in order to see potential hazards early.

21-7. It can frustrate other drivers and make them angry.

21-8. Merging vehicles at on-ramps.

21-9. At or near the same speed as the freeway traffic.

21-10. Make room for merging traffic, if possible.

21-11. You are driving in an exit lane.

21-12. Only if you are carrying the minimum number of persons shown on the sign.

21-13. Change lanes one at a time until you are in the proper lane.

21-14. There is a merging lane ahead.

21-15. You could be cited for driving too slowly, if you block the normal and reasonable flow of traffic.

21-16. At or near the same speed as the freeway traffic.

22-1. License Information, proof of insurance, vehicle registration, and current address.

22-2. Move your vehicle out of the traffic lane if possible.

22-3. $750.

22-4. There is an injury or death.

22-5. Flash your brake lights or turn on your emergency flashers.

22-6. Leave a note on the vehicle and report the accident to city police or CHP.

22-7. Turn on your emergency flashers.

23-1. Stop as long as the red lights are flashing.

23-2. No, it is illegal.

23-3. At all times.

23-4. Front seat, airbags.

23-5. Only if the child is supervised by a person 12 years or older.

23-6. False.

24-1. Paper or electronic.

24-2. If you are over 18 and it is voice-operated hands-free operation.

24-3. Hybrid or low emission.

24-4. License plates.

25-1. 15 mph.

25-2. 15 mph.

25-3. Dumping or abandoning an animal on a highway.

25-4. Yes, because he or she is under 60 pounds.

25-5. 15 mph.

25-6. Within 18 inches.

25-7. 0.08% (eight hundredths of one percent) or higher.

25-8. Only if the animals are properly secured.

25-9. 25 mph.

25-10. A 3-axle vehicle if the Gross Vehicle Weight is less than 6,000 pounds.

25-11. Sell or transfer your vehicle.

25-12. At least 4-second gap in traffic.

25-13. Extending more than 4 feet from your rear bumper.

25-14. 15mph.

25-15. Jailed in the county jail for not more than 1 year.

25-16. 25 mph.

25-17. 11 PM and 5AM.

ABOUT THE AUTHOR

Richard P. Clem is an author and attorney in Minneapolis, Minnesota. His books include study guides which narrow down the exact information required for the exam. This book is constantly being updated. If you take the test and it includes material that was not in this book, please let the author know at clem.law@usa.net.

Made in the USA
San Bernardino, CA
06 April 2018